Praise for *Tr...*

"Rayona Sharpnack offers a compas[...] edged change. Her understanding [...] context, behavior, impact, and engagement is backed by compelling human examples. Read this book to understand your past and shape a future as successful as your dreams."

> —Swanee Hunt, director of the Women and Public Policy Program at Harvard's Kennedy School of Government and U.S. Ambassador to Austria (1993–1997)

"A thoughtful consideration of the ways in which our personal lives and our lives as leaders intersect."

> —Barbara Kellerman, Kennedy School of Government, Harvard University

"Based on her wealth of experience in coaching both men and women leaders, Rayona Sharpnack shows us how we can go deeper, to the hidden obstacles that stand in the way of real personal growth. *Trade Up!* is an invaluable guide for empowerment and success."

> —Riane Eisler, author of *The Chalice and the Blade* and *The Real Wealth of Nations*

"Rayona Sharpnack has written an absolutely brilliant new book called *Trade Up!* Her insight and wisdom are absolutely on the mark. This book will catapult anyone who reads it to a whole new level of leadership and power. Rayona has such a bounty of profound wisdom in this book that it is overflowing with gem after gem after gem. She is a mistress of context and language and will empower you to take your organization, your people, your mission, and your life to unprecedented levels of effectiveness, clarity, and excellence. *Trade Up!* is brilliantly written, and eminently wise, highly practical and deeply inspiring. Buy it, read it, and share it with everyone you know."

> —Lynne Twist, author and founder of the Soul of Money Institute

"*Trade Up!* reminds us that context is everything in life and shapes the way we see and act in the world. Whether you are transforming your workplace, your community, or your life, this book is a great roadmap and sustenance for the journey."

—Susan Burnett, senior vice president, talent management, Gap Inc.

"*Trade Up!* is an eye-opening, mind-expanding guide to more effective leadership and a rewarding life. Everyone can reap the benefits!"

—Adrienne Hall, president/CEO, the Hall Group

JB JOSSEY-BASS

Trade Up!

Five Steps for Redesigning Your Leadership and Life from the Inside Out

Rayona Sharpnack

John Wiley & Sons, Inc.

Copyright © 2007 by Rayona Sharpnack

Published by Jossey-Bass
A Wiley Imprint
989 Market Street, San Francisco, CA 94103-1741   www.josseybass.com

Wiley Bicentennial logo: Richard J. Pacifico

No part of this publication may be reproduced, stored in a retrieval system, or transmitted
in any form or by any means, electronic, mechanical, photocopying, recording, scanning,
or otherwise, except as permitted under Section 107 or 108 of the 1976 United States
Copyright Act, without either the prior written permission of the publisher, or authorization
through payment of the appropriate per-copy fee to the Copyright Clearance Center, Inc.,
222 Rosewood Drive, Danvers, MA 01923, 978-750-8400, fax 978-646-8600, or on the Web
at www.copyright.com. Requests to the publisher for permission should be addressed to the
Permissions Department, John Wiley & Sons, Inc., 111 River Street, Hoboken, NJ 07030,
201-748-6011, fax 201-748-6008, or online at www.wiley.com/go/permissions.

Readers should be aware that Internet Web sites offered as citations and/or sources for further
information may have changed or disappeared between the time this was written and when it
is read.

Limit of Liability/Disclaimer of Warranty: While the publisher and author have used their
best efforts in preparing this book, they make no representations or warranties with respect
to the accuracy or completeness of the contents of this book and specifically disclaim any
implied warranties of merchantability or fitness for a particular purpose. No warranty may
be created or extended by sales representatives or written sales materials. The advice and
strategies contained herein may not be suitable for your situation. You should consult with a
professional where appropriate. Neither the publisher nor author shall be liable for any loss
of profit or any other commercial damages, including but not limited to special, incidental,
consequential, or other damages.

Jossey-Bass books and products are available through most bookstores. To contact Jossey-Bass
directly call our Customer Care Department within the U.S. at 800-956-7739, outside the
U.S. at 317-572-3986, or fax 317-572-4002.

Jossey-Bass also publishes its books in a variety of electronic formats. Some content that
appears in print may not be available in electronic books.

Library of Congress Cataloging-in-Publication Data
Sharpnack, Rayona.
   Trade up! : five steps for redesigning your leadership and life from the inside out / Rayona
Sharpnack.
      p. cm.
   Includes bibliographical references and index.
   ISBN 978-1-118-76733-7 (pbk)
  1. Leadership.   2. Success in business.   I. Title.
   HD57.7.S4763 2007
   658.4'092—dc22

                                                                    2007024588

FIRST EDITION
HB Printing   10 9 8 7 6 5 4 3 2
PB Printing   10 9 8 7 6 5 4 3 2 1

Dedicated to Nanny, Mother, Raven, and
Chelsea . . . four generations of women who loved me without
reservation and taught me the power of "Trading Up!"

Contents

Trade Up!

INTRODUCTION: BEYOND BUSINESS AS USUAL

> I think most of us are looking for a calling, not a
> job. Most of us, like the assembly line worker, have
> jobs that are too small for our spirit. Jobs are not big
> enough for people.
>
> —*Nora Watson*

Are you a sucker for a heartwarming story?

The great stories in life are about triumph or victory over difficult circumstances. As readers, movie watchers, and followers of the news, we love to cheer for a hero or heroine as he or she overcomes adversity and wins. We watch in wonder as Luke Skywalker transitions from sullen teenager to Jedi knight in *Star Wars* or an unhappy and disconnected family learns to sing beautifully together in *The Sound of Music*. We cheer as underdog sports teams like the 1954 Hoosiers or the 2006 New Orleans Saints surpass every expectation but their own. We are inspired by leaders and public figures who overcome personal challenges or difficult times to make a difference in the world.

What we love about such stories is the sense that the people in them have "traded up." Rather than stay mired in the part of their lives that's not working, they trade up to a new mind-set or point of view that helps them achieve their dreams and goals. They don't abandon "who they are" when they arrive at this fork in the road; in fact, they feel more integrated and comfortable with themselves than they ever have before. Nor do they abandon their loved ones and friends to make it. Indeed, in the process of trading up, the people I work with and the people I've observed from a distance become better family members, friends, or colleagues, strengthening and reinforcing their relationships rather than dissolving them. They discover that flying solo is a no-win proposition and that it takes love and support from others to succeed in a meaningful and impactful way.

It's easy to view such stories as rare moments of wonder, but in fact, "trading up" happens around us all the time. It's happened to you at those times in your life when you faced difficulties or strife or struggled to achieve a dream or goal. It happens to friends, family members, and colleagues. It happens to schools and communities, and teams and businesses. We don't always notice these trade-ups because we don't have the language to point them out. And because we lack the language, we don't understand the journey that each person or group undergoes in the process; nor do we know how to mark, measure, or celebrate the victories that result.

This book is about understanding the language of trading up and learning its methodology so that you can put it into practice where you need it most. You may be doing this for an aspect of your own life or for the sake of your children or partner. You may be doing it to help your community or your business or your nonprofit organization achieve its goals. In whatever area you want to trade up, I guarantee you'll be making your life richer and the world a better place as a result. The question isn't, Can you solve your problems and achieve your goals? The question is, How good are you willing to let life be?

Contextual Thinking, Not Wishful Thinking

When people, particularly leaders, learn how to deliberately trade up, they come to rely on a set of tools and processes to effect the desired change. Doing so, they confront the confusion, struggle, and challenge of life and combine it with opportunity, hard work, and focus to achieve a lofty goal and have an impact on the world. Trading up is not about engaging in wishful thinking. No one makes a significant change in their lives or in the lives of others by merely wishing good things to happen. If so, the world would be a paradise.

And yet, the nature of your *thinking* and how you articulate your dreams and goals to yourself and others has a major impact on your chances of success. The game is played in the mind, first and foremost, and language is the critical instrument. In this book, you will learn a great deal about language and its power to transform reality. Some of the concepts and terms may be very new to you, or are used in new ways, though they will come to seem simple, natural, and self-evident when you grow accustomed to them. In a way, it's like the first time you learn how to play a musical instrument, speak a foreign language, or use algebra or a computer. What seems mysterious and otherworldly becomes ordinary and unconscious as the pathways of the brain get modified or rewired. Practice is essential. Results depend on the effort and attention that you invest. Having a good teacher or a good guidebook makes a major difference.

My good friend Marilyn King was just an "ordinary gal," in her words, who decided that she wanted to be an Olympic athlete. She succeeded—twice. Of course, she did not achieve that lofty standard of athletic performance by snapping her fingers; a whole set of deliberate choices and mental and physical practices supported and enabled her goal. But the journey started with a decision that her dream was possible, and that mental leap is no small matter. She needed to trade up from a belief that she was just an "ordinary gal" to the belief that she was a person who had the potential to compete on the world's most vaunted stage. Then she needed to follow through in both word and deed. In Munich in

1972, and in Montreal in 1976, she competed in the grueling pentathlon. In 1979, a car accident rendered her physically unable to train. Rather than accept that setback as a dead end, she explored and utilized techniques from the nascent field of mental training to place second at the Olympic trials for the 1980 Moscow games. Moving on from her athletic career, Marilyn reinvented herself again as a corporate coach and inspirational speaker. Her focus on world peace has led to work with the foremost leaders in the world and two invitations to speak at the United Nations. Not bad for an ordinary gal.

A newer friend, Erin Gruwell, helped not only herself but a classroom of underprivileged inner-city high school students to trade up. You can watch Erin's story in the 2007 feature film, *The Freedom Writers*, where she is played by Academy Award–winning actress Hilary Swank. Her first trade-up was a decision she made, while watching the Rodney King riots on TV, to forego law school and become a teacher. Next, when she was assigned a student teaching position at an inner-city high school, she found herself in a difficult classroom environment overcrowded with students who had been written off by the educational system. She could have accepted the universally held premise that those students were unteachable, but instead, she treated them as gifted human beings with rich stories to tell and experiences to share. Her students came together like a family, visited the U.S. Congress to testify about their lives, and went on to university and graduate school. As a leader-educator, Erin helped a group of young people trade up to a better vision of themselves and helped other educators understand what was possible when prescribed limitations are challenged. The diligence and effort required cannot be overstated, but the journey began when Erin challenged assumptions and articulated a different kind of conversation.

Sometimes the world seems like it has been and always will be set in its ways; then someone nudges our beliefs or opens our eyes, and a whole new universe of possibility becomes available. That's what trading up can do for individuals, organizations, and societies. On a corporate or organizational front, we see a trade-up to new products or new ways of doing business transform habits and possibilities regularly. Once upon a time, no one thought anyone would buy a $500 portable music system; then came Apple's iPod, which brought computer software, digital technology, fashionable design, and home entertainment into one appealing device, reviving a company and transforming the online music and video industries. Once upon a time, development and charity work in the Third World focused on huge expensive programs and projects. Then came 2006 Nobel Peace Prize–winner Muhammad Yunus, a professor of economics in Bangladesh, who founded a bank that made microloans of as little as $1 to women for start-up businesses. Those cottage industries had tremendous impact on local communities, and the idea revolutionized development strategies. Similarly, in the area of health philanthropy, people like Bill and Melinda Gates have focused on small projects and test cases to find practical solutions for diseases that were largely ignored in the past, in the process greatly improving the quality of life for many people. Those changes started with a departure in conventional thinking, communicated through language and reinforced by consistent action, that had an impact on achieving a goal or dream.

Socially, I can think of many trade-ups we've seen in recent years. For example, a generation ago, men in this country were relegated to being the sole breadwinners in the family unit. Now, stay-at-home dads are plentiful, and the option provides great flexibility for families and a special experience for men that greatly enhances the quality of child rearing. What started as an impossibility or even a taboo becomes acceptable and encouraged through a change in language. Similarly, twenty years ago, women in top executive ranks were few and far between. Now they run some of the largest organizations in the world. Meanwhile, male leaders, once prided on their toughness and command-and-control mentality, are being valued for their emotional intelligence and their skills at relationship building. A few years back, the conversation in the NFL—a sport I follow with great interest—concerned the lack of opportunity for African

American coaches. In 2007, we had two African American coaches competing for the Super Bowl.

When we trade up from an intractable or "stuck" perspective to a better and more invigorating one, we are changing or shifting something I call "context." In trading up, Marilyn King shifted her context from ordinary gal to Olympic athlete. Erin Gruwell traded up from a sympathetic observer of social disenfranchisement to an empowering educator. Muhammad Yunus traded up from a caring economics professor with few resources to a banker engaged in affecting significant change at the community level.

"Shifting context" is a critical phrase to understand. Most of us carry our context around subconsciously, without realizing how it limits our actions and choices, our sense of possibility, and even the opportunities that come to us. When we trade up, we abandon one context for another one that we create deliberately in order to get what we want out of life.

But what exactly is context? Can I see it or touch it? As we use the term in this book, *context* is the often *unexamined mind-set or frame of reference we operate from that informs our behavior and evokes behavior from others.* In other words, context is the belief system you carry inside. It's your frame of reference, your paradigm, your view of reality or of life from which your actions and behaviors spring. Context is usually something you have inherited or have had impressed upon you in your formative years, not something you have consciously developed for yourself. Much of it comes "loaded at the factory"; it's the default setting that your brain and spirit automatically return to, especially in moments of crisis or fatigue.

Groups, organizations, and societies have contexts, too—the culture or set of norms and beliefs that provide the boundaries of acceptable behavior and predictable outcomes. Now, that may sound strange because organizations don't actually think, but organizations do have atmospheres, environments, or cultures that enlarge or suppress what people are allowed to think, say, and do, whether they recognize it or not.

Context shapes everything we see or do, as individuals and social beings. It shapes who "you be" as a person. Yes, you have physical attributes that distinguish you, but ultimately, *what makes you unique is the configuration of preconceived ideas that constitute your reality.* Wow, read that last sentence three times slowly!

Consider the idea that the world is filled with an infinite number of facts we can use to reinforce our beliefs and decide our actions. Why do you choose to think and do one thing instead of another? You probably feel that your choices are based on a conscious sorting out of the available options. Actually, you are usually seeking confirming evidence for that which you are predisposed to believe is true. As a simple example, for thousands of years people saw the sun rise every morning in the East, travel overhead during the day, and disappear every evening into the horizon in the West. Naturally, most people—and most societies—believed it was obvious that the sun revolved around the Earth. This view nicely supported the belief that God created man as the center of the Universe. When Copernicus and Galileo offered contrary evidence, the news was not received well. In fact, their view created a scientific, spiritual, and social revolution that we are still grappling with in many ways.

Context is the preestablished belief system you use to interpret and move through every situation you encounter. It ignites the automatic reaction you have when you don't have the option of making your response a conscious one. Although we like to think that we get wiser and more deliberate about our choices, reactions, and actions as we get older, our built-in context doesn't leave a lot of room for new behavior because it's cluttered with perceptions inherited from our families, society, friends, partners, and other outside influences. In return, when other people—those friends, family members, political leaders, and colleagues—tell you what is or isn't right, they are speaking from *their* contexts. Sometimes this context is at odds with your own, and the two of you may as well be coming from two different planets like, say . . . Venus and Mars.

As human beings we have a natural and very powerful tendency to hold onto our contexts as though they were life itself. Think about the most certain beliefs that you hold and how real, immutable, and factual they feel to you. You may even know lots of people who support those beliefs, confirming that they are reality. In actuality, whatever view of reality you hold is only a *conclusion* you have adopted somewhere along the journey of life. Other people hold very different perspectives of what is or is not real.

Contexts are almost entirely made up of conclusions—what I consider dead-end *interpretations of reality masquerading as fact*— that limit or restrict what we are able to see, think, or talk about. For instance, the idea that humans could never travel to the moon or a woman or African American could never be president of the United States are ideas that once had the ring of truth, when in fact they were limiting perceptions of reality masked as truth.

Conclusions include everything from perceptions to interpretations to beliefs, rumors, and much more. Individual contexts— sets of conclusions—come from a variety of places: our families, our ethnic or cultural backgrounds, the areas of the world or the time in which we are raised, our educational experiences, and virtually everything we absorb from our environments on a day-to-day basis. Organizational contexts arise initially from the founders' personal contexts but then morph over time as economic factors, changes in the industry and market, and financial influences like Wall Street and government regulations, as well as shifts in personnel at the top, have an impact.

Why should you care about what context or set of conclusions make up your reality? We care because context is what determines our actions and behaviors. For example, if Sonia's context is, "I know more about leadership than my colleague," Sonia probably exhibits behaviors and has conversations that validate her view. Whether she's conscious of it or not, she looks for and finds flaws in how her colleague does her job. She probably gossips about other people's insufficiencies. Sonia's view is influential on her behavior because, in her mind, her context is a set of conclusions about the very nature of reality that has the power of truth. Sonia even thinks she is doing the right thing by pointing out deficiencies in others and working past their faults to accomplish her objectives. Chances are, however, unless you are Sonia, you don't like working with her. I bet Sonia's team, organization, and even family suffer as a result.

Pain Points: The Great Motivator of Change

Why should Sonia stop to question her own context and engage in deliberately trying to build a new one? Most likely, the only reason Sonia would be motivated to effect such change is if she has been confronted by some failure of her own or has caused some pain in others that forces her to make a change. As human beings, we do not change easily or willingly. But we are capable of making great transformative shifts when we need to trade up.

I can think of at least two big reasons why you're reading this book. The first possibility is that there's something in your life— some person, situation, or problem—that's causing you suffering. The second possibility is that you want to create, make, or change something so much it hurts. That's okay. The catch-22 of life is that we're rarely motivated to evolve unless we're uncomfortable, threatened, desperate, or fed up with the status quo. The evolution itself is the art of trading up.

Let's call those forms of suffering "pain points." We've all got them. I've got mine and you've got yours. Even the most composed and successful people you've ever met or read about have theirs. You may have a family member, neighbor, or colleague who's a constant source of irritation or frustration. You may work for a company or a community group that is not open to operating or changing the way you think it should. Or you may even have an aspect of your own personality—your weight, health, or finances; the way you present yourself or come across; the intractable limits of your career—that you'd like to fix or that other people are begging you to change. On the other hand, you may be a dreamer or visionary who's out to accomplish something that seems highly unlikely or nearly impossible. Or you may just be someone who has always wanted to become a better person but lacks the know-how, role model, or inspiration to trade up.

Pain points hurt because they matter. If they were easy to resolve, we'd snap our fingers, absorb their lessons, and rise above them. As a busy person, with more on your plate than you can juggle on a good day, you're probably not reading this book to dwell on your problems, failings, or disappointments. You spend enough time in that swamp already. Rather, you're standing in the self-help or leadership section of the bookstore because you want some damn answers! You want some guidance on juggling the demands of being a parent, friend, or human being while somehow surviving the demands of corporate America. You want some approaches and tools for leading your group, team, or community. You want a parents' "How-to" manual for understanding and influencing your children, or a personal "How-to" manual for reducing the stress you're experiencing in your work, marriage, partnership, or life. You want to understand what other people are thinking. You want to understand how what you say and do is impacting other people. You want to figure out how to play better with others and get on the same wavelength without sacrificing what's really important to you.

You don't want to be a victim, but you feel like one sometimes. You don't want to make excuses, but you're sick of the pieces not falling into place. You're tired of running hard just to keep up. You no longer want to pay such a high price for success. You want some forward momentum. You want some real progress. You want the wind at your back for a change.

I'm never going to say that you're wrong or argue that those emotions should be treated lightly—but I am going to say some things that you might resist hearing at first. The truth is, fixing it or them is rarely the answer. How many times has it worked before? Recall for one blissful moment the last time you changed a loved one's behavior or way of thinking. Tell me about the day you convinced some colleague, boss, or team of the rightness of your argument and really saw the point stick. If you're like most people, you don't have many good examples to provide. Even the rare victories probably came at great cost.

Spinning Your Wheels Versus Getting Traction

If you're utterly sick of pushing your shoulder up against the immoveable stone, I'd like to posit a different solution. Just for now, consider the possibility that it's not about *them* or *it*. Instead, let's think about *you*. Whether you are most concerned about your child, your partner, your colleague, your organization, or some corner of the world, your ability to have a positive leadership impact depends a lot more on who you are *being* than what you are *doing*.

The important question you need to ask yourself is not whether your view of reality is right or wrong, good or bad, but whether your view of reality is helping or hindering you in your life or circumstances. Your context, set of conclusions, belief system, or frame of reference might have carried you for quite some time in supporting your relationships and helping you achieve your goals. But what worked for us once doesn't always provide what we need now. Strengths can become weaknesses as circumstances change. There may come a phase in your life, or you may face situations on a day-to-day basis, where your factory-installed context actually prevents you from getting what you want, no matter how badly you want it. Those moments are the pain points I mentioned. When you are frustrated or suffering with your inability to get your family members or colleagues to see the facts as you do and behave accordingly, or when the world does not seem to fall into place the way you want or need it to in order to achieve your goals, chances are it is because the context you are working from is getting in the way.

It is possible, however, to choose your context deliberately in order to operate from a view of reality that gets you what you want and need. I call this "the art of trading up." Doing so requires a five-step process that we work through in detail over the course of this book. The journey requires that you first uncover or reveal

Figure I.1 Reveal and Shift Context

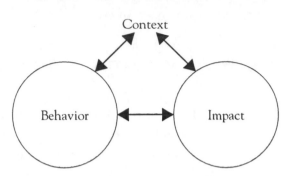

the context you are operating from before you can create, design, or trade up to a context that will clear the way for new choices or behaviors that serve you better. The power of revealing context provides you with the awareness to choose to keep it, discard it, or trade up for one you actually want (see Figure I.1).

What context is shaping or limiting who you are, what you do, what you think, and how you act with others? A set of automatic responses are triggered whenever you are unconscious of the beliefs or perspectives you hold. It is only by digging within ourselves and working with the support of others that we can bring to the surface those deeply held beliefs and choose better ones. People who do so are released to view the world in incredibly freeing ways. They connect readily to themselves and to a higher purpose. That's why context shifting is such an important aspect of leadership. Once a person connects with her passion and recognizes that it cannot be created in isolation, that person becomes a real leader, connecting with and helping to transform others, drawing the like-minded to her cause. The game of life was never meant to be played solo. The creativity, energy, and enthusiasm of engagement is the payback of leadership and one of the most fulfilling experiences in life. It starts and ends with you, but in the process it embraces the world. As a leader, what is it that you want to change or do? How badly do you want it? Do you have any idea how much impact you can really have? It doesn't start with it or them—it starts with you. This book describes the process by which you can uncover how you be in the world—meaning *how your current context affects your behavior and impact*—and trade up to a more useful context to achieve what you want. What you discover about yourself during that journey will surprise you.

What is the pain or possibility that makes you want to change?

Nose to the Grindstone

In the chapters that follow, you will meet many people who have traded up by revealing and shifting context in themselves and others. You will read about their pain points, learn what they discovered about themselves and the people around them, and see what they did to change the rules of the game. But to give you an initial picture of the journey you will undertake in shifting your own context, let me first tell you about some work that I've been doing to transform my life.

To say that I've been driven and worked hard in my life is an understatement. I was raised in a lower-middle-class family in Nevada with three older brothers I had to wrestle down to get the extra slice of meatloaf. For some reason, I never saw my gender or age as a barrier to what I wanted to do. In fourth grade I decided to become a physical education teacher, long before such a position had been created for women in my town, and I held true to that vision through college. When I was eleven years old, I became a national record holder in the Junior Olympics for the longest softball throw. At sixteen I won the Nevada singles and doubles tennis championship. During college, while playing three sports, I soaked up everything I could about linguistics, business, athletics, psychology, and education. Consumed by my love for ideas, I believed I could change the world.

After college, I ventured into the Amateur Athletic Association (AAA) and professional softball. In 1978, while playing professionally for the International Women's Softball League, I led a strike against the owners of the San Jose franchise because of their questionable business practices. When I took the reins of that franchise, I became one of the first player–general managers in professional sports and led that team to record on-field and financial performance.

When the league folded, and I left professional sports behind, I became the softball coach at Stanford University while still maintaining my junior high school teaching job. After eleven years I was frustrated with the education system's resistance to innovation. Knowing that leadership was really my calling, I became a business consultant. I brought my experience in athletics, business, and teaching; my academic work in linguistics and psychology; and the social-psychology theories I'd picked up from my friend and mentor Virginia Satir to problems facing the corporate world. One of my first challenges arose at Sun Microsystems, then one of the powerhouses in the emerging high-tech revolution. Meeting with female employees at Sun and at other Bay Area companies, I heard about the inequities and unrewarded contributions women were making in the workplace. My previous work with in-house leaders shone a light on those problems and helped catalyze organizational change. The consulting projects kept coming, and I continued working in increasingly more complex, more challenging, and more rewarding situations. Along the way, I raised my daughter and continued to be active in sports, associations, volunteer work, and teaching.

Longing to share the work I was doing inside organizations with more women, I formed the Institute for Women's Leadership (IWL) and began conducting three-day workshops with powerful women for some of the most important organizations in America and abroad. High achievers, the women who come to me typically feel stretched beyond capacity by the needs of family, the urge to be more healthy and fulfilled personally, and the intense demands of high-profile corporate positions. Such women are seeking breakthrough change, and I help to guide them through the process of unlearning what they assume to be true about their worlds and reorienting their focus and approach. The conversations we generate change the way these women think about their leadership, allowing them to scale their passion and skills beyond what they could have imagined, while simultaneously reconnecting with their inner needs. One of the great satisfactions in that work for me is seeing those leaders develop relationships that go beyond the workshops, creating a network of engaged women who support each other's personal and professional objectives while furthering their influence across industries and communities.

All of this sounds wonderful, even to me, but it took its toll. My mother passed away. My health became an issue. I was getting intense headaches that wouldn't stop. My organization had increased in size and I was feeling the stress and burden of its upkeep. I was suffering in large ways and small.

During a session with my own executive coach, Ellen Wingard, I elaborated on those many woes and gave her my latest poor-me story. Ellen, who is very patient but very provocative, said that my complaints sounded familiar, like a tune I'd been humming for some time. I stopped to consider where those feelings were coming from. When I thought about it, I recognized that the sense of suffering and sacrifice, and the feeling of futility that drove me to work like a dog was nothing new—in fact, I'd been like that for as long as I could remember. Perhaps that was a context I was operating from, a reality that I'd been programmed to believe in rather than an objective reality itself. Over the ensuing weeks, those ideas remained active in the back of my brain, as I recalled how I'd been raised and how that had influenced my outlook on life. Indeed, I realized I'd been hardwired to work myself into the ground.

When I tried to capture that context in words, the expression "I'll never get anywhere in life if I don't keep my nose to the grindstone" quickly came to mind. As a phrase it seems fairly innocent, but as a belief system it had been embedded in my personality for fifty-one years. I knew that *nose to the grindstone* had long been a useful belief for me, leading to a lot of success in life. But in recent years I had gone from thinking that hard work was important to

Figure I.2   Nose to the Grindstone

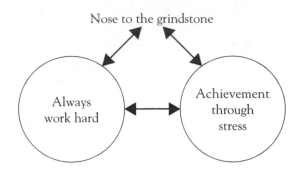

believing that *everything* had to be hard work (see Figure I.2). I paid a serious personal price for this approach, overdoing it on the trade-offs and sacrifices, selling myself short in terms of the enjoyment and satisfaction that makes life fun and worthwhile.

Once I became conscious of the fact that *I'll never get anywhere in life if I don't keep my nose to the grindstone* was a prevailing context in my life, I was able to see that nothing would really change for me until I changed that deeply embedded view. As you will learn through this book, one of the keys to changing our thinking—and thereby changing our behaviors—is to first change the language we use. "Nose to the grindstone" was a phrase describing the way I had always been; I needed to come up with a new phrase that described the person I wanted to become.

Of course, being a nose-to-the-grindstone person, I worked like a dog to think of something that would suit me better. I knew from my experience working with other people that I couldn't swing the pendulum to the other extreme and become laid-back Rayona just because that idea sounded appealing. The change had to be part of me, a discovery or, more accurately, a new invention.

Shifting to Grace and Ease

I hope this makes intuitive sense to you. No person or organization can radically transform their personality or culture just because it seems fitting to do so. Unless the seeds of that change aren't already inherent, the new incarnation will be unsustainable. I knew that any phrase capturing the compelling future I wanted to pledge myself to would have to resonate in my body, striking a physical and spiritual chord as it made itself known to me.

I woke up in the middle of the night a few weeks later with the phrase "grace and ease" in my mind. I liked those words a lot. *Grace and ease.* If grace and ease was a way to live, I wanted some of that. The more I thought about "grace and ease," the more it resonated with me, and I settled on it. I knew I had to turn it into a conclusion in order to make it useful for having an impact on my life, so I elaborated on it to the point where I had a new context: *It all turns out with grace and ease.* I rolled that around in my brain over the ensuing days, feeling as though it gave me everything I wanted. I could still have my ambition and drive, but I didn't need to work or stress so hard anymore for the results. After all, I was now committed that *it all turns out with grace and ease.*

The next step for me was to begin a process of being deliberately conscious of my new context (see Figure I.3). Nose-to-the-grindstone behaviors and attitudes were not easy to drop. I couldn't rid myself of them the way I might send a closetful of old clothes to Goodwill. Mentally, every time I relapsed into my nose-to-the-grindstone ways, I'd stop and think, "It all turns out with grace and ease." Despite my best intentions, I often realized after the fact that I'd been

Figure I.3   It All Turns Out with Grace and Ease

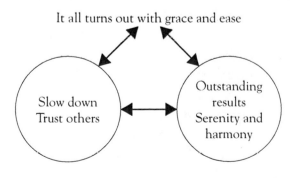

putting my nose to the grindstone, and I would let myself know that consciously. Recognizing the experience of putting my nose to the grindstone near or around the time it took place helped ease my burden just a little bit, and I was able to remind myself, "It all turns out with grace and ease."

As you will discover for yourself, it wasn't enough for me to go it alone in this work of context shifting—I needed the help of the people around me. I enlisted my staff at my organization, my friends, and my daughter and asked them to let me know when I was behaving in ways that typified my nose-to-the-grindstone mode. It goes without saying that they knew what that behavior looked like and were able to act as my outside mirror in pointing it out. I also asked the people around me to let me know when they saw some of that grace and ease I was aiming for. They had fun doing that, and it became a way to pat ourselves on the back when things around us worked or when my many projects went smoothly and seamlessly without the effort and stress we were all accustomed to.

Trading up is a full makeover. The transformation doesn't stop in your mind, but extends outward to your relationships and community, and inward to your body. For these reasons, during this time I also worked on my health. Everyone knows that the secret to weight loss is more calories out, fewer calories in. But although I'd been an athlete most of my life, once my playing days were over I was like many athletes in despising exercise for its own sake. It wasn't easy for me to imagine running, biking, or tread-milling just to get in shape, but I did like to walk. When I started doing my power walks, the boredom and physical strain struck me as a grind, so I began to say my gratitude prayers along the way. I started by thanking my own body, literally moving up from my feet to my head, and that got me to travel a certain distance with more grace and ease, while also putting me into closer connection with my physical self. I moved beyond my body and began thanking the people around me and other aspects of my life and the world. Before I knew it, the act of getting in shape had been transformed for me from dreary exercise to a chance to reflect and connect on the wonder of life and my presence in it. A bit more grace and ease set in—literally becoming embedded in my body.

Little by little, my new context took hold. I started seeing the results in my work, my relationships, and my life. As leader of my organization, for instance, the context of grace and ease was a relief to all, since it helped lower the stress and pressure we felt. It also freed people up to become better leaders in their own right. Part of my reaction in nose-to-the-grindstone mode was always to take responsibility for everyone's work. Resisting quick fixes whenever crises developed and seeing more opportunities to problem-solve allowed me to back off, while the people who worked for me were groomed to take on roles of greater responsibility. It sounds simple, but it was a culture change that created business opportunities as well as personal ones. Moreover, it was sustainable, and it often surprised us in its impact and influence. Whatever air we were breathing seemed to affect others too. When the group of senior women leaders in our leadership forums began meeting outside their programs to further their relationships, engage in each other's leadership concerns, and deepen the influence of their collective might, it was a wonderful sign to me that I did not have to hoist every block in whatever cathedral I was involved in building. The proof was all around me. It really does turn out with grace and ease.

Carbon Versus Conclusion

Everyone I work with comes to me with some kind of pain point, an aspect of their life they want to transform. Before we can talk about making a change, however, we need to examine the underlying assumptions and perspectives reinforcing, if not creating, the circumstances causing the pain. In other words, we need to understand and articulate the leader's personal context before we can begin to assess whether it's working and then trade up to something more helpful or worthy.

You may find it amazing to learn that the tools of such transformation are mere words. And yet, it is through words that human beings assign meaning to things and thereby interpret or understand the world. (Indeed, some would even go so far as to say it is through words that we "create" the world.) If you don't believe me, imagine how life would be without language. Or, since you can't possibly imagine being language-less, consider how Helen Keller's world opened up when language became available to her. One day, she realized that the motions her teacher, Anne Sullivan, was making on her skin while running water over her hand symbolized the idea of water. Frantically, Helen proceeded to ask Sullivan the names of everything else around her. It was as if by being able to name things, she could "see" them for the first time. She would go on to learn how to speak and hear English using the Tadoma method and pick up four other languages while writing several books and becoming a world-famous spokesperson for various causes.

Language is the means by which we perceive, translate, and understand the world around us, bringing external "reality" into our internal experience of it. Words are the DNA of thought. In the Book of Genesis, God gives Adam the power to name all of the plants and animals in the Garden of Eden, making him master over all other creatures. The Taoists believe that it is only through the naming of things that we distinguish individual objects from infinity and give them shape and definition. The poets understand this. The novelist A. S. Byatt says we are language animals. Once we have the power of language, everything is transformed. Helen Keller was able to turn her knowledge of the word *water* into five languages and then leadership in a number of important causes. Once you "get" language you can apply it to anything. You can use the same words to talk with a store clerk, express love to your partner, teach a child, recite poetry, build a power plant, or define a vision that will motivate others to achieve a goal. In a similar way, zeroes and ones are the DNA of our digital era, allowing us to run computer programs, send e-mail, communicate with colleagues while traveling halfway around the world, shop, download music, and view photographs of our loved ones anywhere anytime.

Are You Creating or Describing Reality?

But what does language actually do? It's worth understanding this in more depth. Language's first function is to describe or label things. In other words, language has a *descriptive* property that allows you to look around and say, this is a cat, that is a tree, this is a molecule of sodium, that is a feeling called grief. In fact, the more abstract a concept becomes, the more useful and powerful language gets. Without a word called *grief*, would we be able to define the feeling that overcomes us when we experience significant loss? I'm not sure if we could. There are feelings expressed in some languages, for example, that don't have easy equivalents in others. The Japanese have a word, *natsukashii*, that could perhaps best be translated into English as "wistful longing" and "a bitter-sweet but comforting remembrance." *Natsukashii* is such a commonly expressed or experienced word in Japan that it helps to describe the national character; yet it has no obvious equivalent in our culture. Does it mean we don't feel such an emotion? To an extent it does. The act of labeling the abstract concept helps to distinguish it from the blur of human emotions, providing it with more tangible reality than it otherwise would have had.

Besides its descriptive property, language also has a *generative* property, meaning that we can use language to describe a future and thereby bring it into reality. Most of us don't realize that language creates the future, but consider some simple common examples. When your sister says, "I'm going to the store," she is setting herself off on a path that will make that future come true. When you stand at the altar and say, "I do," you are committing yourself to a future that is different from the past. In fact, language forces us to make commitments all of the time. Whenever we use language in a generative way, we are committing ourselves to a specific future at the expense of a variety of other possibilities. "I will make vice president by the time I'm thirty" may not instantly transform you into a senior executive in charge of research and development, but if you are serious about that statement it sets you onto a different path than if you said, "I'm content to hold down this desk job until I win the lottery." You will make different choices because of that stated desire, and you will also think about your future differently and come across differently to others.

Now that I've described the distinctions, I'm betting that you can easily think about language in terms of its two properties—descriptive and generative. As language animals, however, we run into problems whenever we believe something is descriptive when it is actually generative. For instance, if I say, "I'm five foot nine and one hundred and forty pounds," that's a *description* of my current physical status. But if I say, "I can never lose weight because I hate exercise," that feels like an accurate description of the truth when it's actually a *conclusion* I've made about the future. Is that future more likely to transpire just because I've stated it in such a way? You bet. Chances are, I'm not going to lose any weight if I tell myself I can't.

Consider the almost infinite number of other small but influential statements you throw around about yourself and your future all the time. "I'm always late." "I can't cook." "I'm good/bad with money." "My father and I don't get along." "We understand each other." "I love you." "She's boring." I call these kinds of generative statements "conclusions" because they create self-fulfilling prophecies. We think they are descriptions of what is true or real, when they are actually conclusions that describe what we expect to happen.

Conclusions are neither good nor bad, right nor wrong. They are a way of interpreting the world and weaving that understanding into a belief system or perspective. As a type of statement, conclusions have an amazingly tight hold over us because they push us to get into line with a particular destiny. Conclusions may not fully and totally dictate what will transpire tomorrow or ten years from now, but they exert a very powerful influence over what will happen. When a female executive says, "I can't make president here because of the glass ceiling," how much of that statement is true and how much is a self-fulfilling conclusion, regardless of the political realities of her company? When a male executive says, "I'd love more work-life balance but the job doesn't allow it," he may be describing the very real pressure he's under, but he's also stating a preset conclusion about what is possible.

As language animals, we are programmed to believe that everything we think or say about ourselves or the world is the truth—a direct expression of reality. Consider the possibility that the only things in this world that are factual are made of carbon: the ground we stand on, the trees we lean against. Everything else—the vast range of intangible thoughts, feelings, beliefs, fears, concepts, and so on—is a perspective of reality or a conclusion in which we are enmeshed. And yet, the degree to which our lives are dominated by these conclusions is amazing. They form the content of the many conversations we have with colleagues, family members, or strangers on the street, and they echo in the ongoing, never-ceasing conversations in our minds. Some of those conclusions are beneficial, positive, and useful. Some are restrictive, negative, and limiting. Love is a conclusion; so is the glass ceiling. Both provide a context from which other conclusions, actions, and behaviors arise. Groups and organizations are no less susceptible to the power of conclusions. Common or shared conclusions get handed down from generation to generation. Families, cultures, and nations have conclusions about themselves, as do companies.

In fact, it can be said that each of us is a web of conclusions. Consider the possibility that everything that we call reality and believe to be true is nothing more than a set of tentative conclusions. Sometimes our web of conclusions support or buttress our lives; at other times the web hems us in, leaving us stuck, unable to break free. By becoming more adept at using the generative power of language, we can learn to choose conclusions that offer us a more desirable future. The future is malleable. We influence it through the language we use like an artist shapes clay. Effective leaders are constantly on the lookout for conclusions masquerading as facts. Today's truth is yesterday's discarded theory; today's heresy is tomorrow's innovation.

Once your personal contexts have been revealed, you can decide whether they support or hinder you in achieving what you really want out of life. This gives you the power to create a compelling future that isn't burdened by the past but is informed by it. No one is talking about miracles. It takes hard, sustained work to make deep changes in attitude and behavior. But it always feels a little miraculous when someone puts words to their new personal context and glimpses the magnificent possibilities that become available.

Thinking About Conclusions

> *Fact:* Anything made of carbon, silicon, and so on; anything that can be captured by video, audio, electronic, or written means
>
> *Conclusion:* Any human interpretation, perception, opinion, or explanation

- What are the conclusions from which I am living my life?
- What conclusions have I made about my future?
- What conclusions am I operating from regarding my team?
- What conclusions am I imposing on others?
- What conclusions do I have about myself, my skills, or my opportunities?

Leadership: Shifting Context in Yourself and Others

I'm betting that you're reading this book not just for your own sake, but for others', too. Your instinct is that you need to change something about yourself in order to lead others more effectively. Let me assure you that you're on the right track. Fundamentally, leaders are in the context-shifting business. They work to reveal and shift context in themselves and others in order to achieve a goal.

Let's think about leadership and what it means. In my view, leaders are visionaries. They speak for and evoke action on behalf of a compelling future. That vision of the future can be about anything—a closer family relationship, an important new product launch, an outreach program for a church or volunteer group, a better score in a school's rating. The scope of leadership can be big or small. In fact, leadership is often most effective when it starts small and scales out to larger realms, including the global. Leadership is always personal because it begins with you and your way of being. You can be drafted into parenthood, management, friendship, or life, but you have to enlist in leadership. When you respond to a call for action or an imperative to reshape some aspect of the world, that decision to step forward and lead is a mindful act requiring you to be deliberate about the way you be with others.

Nevertheless, most of us still think of leadership as a station or position. Not surprisingly, when organizations are looking for leaders they tend to focus on people who have been in the field for the requisite amount of time, worked their way diligently up the ranks, and developed the right skill set. I want to put those notions aside right away. There are ten thousand books on Amazon.com that tell you what you need to experience, know, and do in order to lead more effectively. But it takes more than skill development to influence others and make change happen. In this book, we're working on revealing who you are being—because who you are being is a force that influences and affects everything around you. Once you discover who you are being at the deepest levels, you will be prepared to trade up to become the authentic person you need to be in order to impact the world.

If we are not intentional and deliberate about leadership, there can be a profound gap between what we do and who we be. Imagine a seasoned manager meeting with a sales team to discuss a drop-off in the numbers that needs to be turned around before the end of the quarter. The manager knows everything there is to know about the product. She knows how to assess the market, formulate a strategy, change tactics in midstream, and give a motivational speech. But imagine that, consciously or not, she's also thinking about her team in negative ways. Somewhere in the back of her head, she's saying to herself, "Nobody in here is pulling their weight. I'm carrying all of you. But I need you to execute or I'm going to look bad in front of senior management and miss my year-end bonus." Meanwhile, on the outside, she's explaining, "Yes, the market is a challenge, but our customers need our product. Our sales team is top notch. Let's go out there and hit one out of the park."

It's a simplistic example, but I hope it illustrates a point. The gap between what the manager is authentically thinking or feeling and what the manager is publicly telling her team undermines and distorts everything she is trying to accomplish. If you were in the room with her, you would see that her tone, expression, and energy are at odds with her words. At best, she's presenting an appealing but ultimately hollow façade, one that others may not see through consciously but that fails to connect with them at an authentic level. She is not listening to herself or to the members of her team. She has done nothing to bring to the surface what is really going on in the minds of those she needs to rely on. Instead of trying to understand their questions, she has put her effort into trying to bludgeon and steer them in the direction she wants them to go. She may recognize that she has failed to make a difference, but she knows that she has at least gone through the motions. She is unconsciously operating from a context that if her team fails, it won't be because of her lack of effort. It will be because of their poor performance.

This happens all the time in life, in countless variations. The politician has a personal vision but speaks in canned platitudes and the people tune him out. The father has great concern for his son but communicates that harshly and fails to get through. The head nurse tries to change the type of care the patients on her unit are receiving, but the nurses on her staff remain committed to their routine and quickly revert to old ways. In each case, the impact that could have been made is lost because the leader wasn't able to connect with and influence others.

Imagine, instead, that the sales manager we just talked about brought her team together for the same meeting but carried a different agenda. She opens a frank discussion about their predicament by acknowledging that she has a tendency to grab matters out of other people's hands and carry the load all by herself. But she has a vision of the team in which each member is more independent and responsible, thereby growing in personal success while contributing to extraordinary results. She wants the group to be a model of what a top team can do, emulated around the corporation. She knows that as leader her role in this transformation is critical, especially because her own behavior is blocking the destination she seeks. She wants their input as to whether this is possible, and if so, she wants their help to trade up and keep from reverting to her tendency to hoist the burden onto her back and exclude them from contributing.

I think that the relationships in the room would be improved as a result of this kind of conversation, and better outcomes would follow. The manager has entered the discussion with a different mindset and perspective. Instead of believing that it's all their fault, and no one can do it but her, she's recognized her own role in influencing their behaviors and attitudes. She's now engaging her team in a form of partnership, both to help her be more effective at her job and to help them be a better team. She's inspired them at a more authentic level to think about what they are signing up for and what it's worth. This change in belief isn't cosmetic. It's not driven by a cheery speech or a flashy set of tactics. It comes about through a hard-nosed assessment of what's going on beneath the numbers and an honest answer to a very important question: What am I here to do that will make things better? If the manager takes the time to think about her leadership on a broader scale, she may even realize that she has the capacity to make her home and the world a better place, too.

When does someone decide to become a leader? When the compelling future she cares about is bigger than her comfort with the status quo or her fear of taking risks. Discovering the *why* behind leadership fuels the desire to do. In this book, in order to take the steps necessary to become a leader, the only requirement is that you want a future that isn't predictable from where you are now. The forms this leadership takes are limitless. You can be a parent wondering how to get a child to do his chores; a manager whose team has a challenge that's beyond its current capacity; a CEO who wants to build an organization that outpaces the industry; a nonprofit worker who has a dream for making a community impact; or a human being who wants to rethink the way you approach life because you feel stuck or stalled.

Leadership Can Change a Seemingly Inevitable Future

One of my favorite stories about leadership concerns the *Apollo 13* space mission. You may have seen the movie starring Tom Hanks. On April 13, 1970, a three-man crew aboard the *Apollo 13* spacecraft began their journey to the moon. The next day, 200,000 miles from Earth, the spacecraft experienced a critical incident, inspiring the famous quote, "Houston, we have a problem." Routine systems tests on the spacecraft had ignited an electrical fire that caused an oxygen tank to explode. The damage from the explosion crippled the spacecraft and forced the crew to abort their mission to reach the moon. What's more, they needed to abandon one section of the spacecraft and seek refuge in the lunar module in order to have enough oxygen and power just to survive. The odds of a safe return to Earth seemed impossibly long.

Gene Kranz was the lead flight director at NASA mission control. The explosion aboard *Apollo 13* took place on his watch. His job was to make sure the astronauts had a successful trip, and the ultimate measure of success was bringing them home alive. This challenge was made many times more difficult because of the complications brought on by the explosion. Despite the depletion of oxygen and power, however, Kranz refused to give in to the inevitable, and he refused to let others do the same. At one point, top leaders at NASA were quietly discussing the grim situation within Kranz's earshot. One said, "Not since the fire on the launch pad have we had such a P.R. disaster." Three years before, a fire occurring during the launch of the *Apollo 1* space flight killed all three astronauts on board. The NASA brass believed that *Apollo 13* would be an even worse nightmare because the entire incident would provide a grim spectacle on television for all the world to see, stretched out until the bitter end. Overhearing the remark, Kranz interrupted and said with great sternness and conviction, "Excuse me, sir, with all due respect, I believe this will be our finest hour. We're bringing those men home alive."

As a leader, Kranz refused to accept the foregone conclusion that the men were lost. He knew that such a conclusion was not a fact or a predetermined outcome but simply a belief, a perspective based on opinion. Yes, there were great technical obstacles that lent credence to that belief, but that didn't mean such obstacles could not be overcome. Kranz was able to change the agenda or context from "looming P.R. disaster" to "heroic rescue" by asserting his view that the men would return home alive. He worked at changing negative conclusions repeatedly over the long hours that followed. He enlisted all the engineers at NASA, and even scientists in the Soviet Union were willing to help, despite the Cold War. Each technical problem that arose might have required weeks or months to work out under normal circumstances; but Kranz set an agenda in which those problems got solved in hours. People around the world, scientists and citizens alike, rallied behind the rescue mission and cheered when the lunar module splashed down and the astronauts emerged from the capsule healthy and safe. Kranz made NASA's finest hour a reality.

Fundamentally, Kranz made a decision about who he was going to be as a leader and set a compelling vision for everyone to follow. He refused to go down the rathole of reasonableness that would have allowed for easy excuses. He did not interact with anyone else who held such conclusions, but was rigorous and determined about setting a different agenda. He led by shifting the context in which everyone was functioning.

Other Leaders Who Changed the Future

There are many examples of heralded leaders who have shifted context to achieve visionary ends. John F. Kennedy, of course, was the leader who set the original vision of sending a man to the moon and returning him to Earth safely, saying, "We choose to go to the Moon in this decade and do the other things, not because they are easy, but because they are hard." Six years after his death, the vision was achieved, despite the immense resources and significant technological advances required. It didn't happen merely because Kennedy spoke the words, but because his vision had the power to engage the efforts of many people. Rosa Parks helped catalyze the civil rights movement when she refused to move to the back of the bus and make room so that a white passenger could use her seat. Asked by the arresting officer if she was going to comply, Parks responded, "No, I'm not." Those three words challenged what had been an accepted practice of racism and let the world know that it was no longer tolerable. They inspired thousands and then millions of like-minded people to do their part. On the eve of the Battle of Britain, Winston Churchill faced the possibility of invasion and defeat when he gave his famous speech vowing, "We shall defend our island, whatever the cost may be, we shall fight on the beaches, we shall fight on the landing grounds, we shall fight in the fields and in the streets, we shall fight in the hills; we shall never surrender." Those words helped turn the tide of pessimism and fear and roused the courage of citizens and soldiers to surmount terrible trials.

What is it that leaders do to make a difference? What magic element do they bring to the equation that turns base lead into dazzling gold? How do they change the dynamic of a situation and bring everyone into line and moving in the same direction? The leaders I have studied and worked with are in the context-shifting business. More than anything else, they work on revealing and shifting context in themselves and others. This is true even if they don't use the word *context* or even think of that concept. In changing the agenda,

Gene Kranz, John F. Kennedy, Rosa Parks, and Winston Churchill were attempting to trade up from a context that no longer worked to one we desperately needed.

Transformative Change

In this book, you will meet a host of top leaders and learn how the business of context shifting has freed them to assert leadership in new realms while dramatically improving the meaningfulness of their lives and the quality of their relationships. Among them are Colleen Brophy, a chief of vascular surgery and the founder of two biomedical start-ups, who is working to change the approach that surgeons take with patients; Sally Crawford, the founder of a multimillion-dollar consulting firm, who had not taken a single Thanksgiving holiday in twenty-three years and learned that it was not necessary to work hundred-hour weeks to sustain her business; Gretchen McCoy, who led a complete redesign of Visa's global billing system for 21,000 member financial institutions; and Kavita Ramdas, the director of the Global Fund for Women, who is revolutionizing her organization's philanthropic efforts in the developing world.

None of these leaders achieved their grand visions without profound personal change at the deepest levels. Their motivation for initiating such change was not kick-started by their visions, but by the mundane and simple moments that frustrated them or caused them pain. It's rarely the gigantic things that get in our way. Our suffering or pain points usually come down to the minor conflicts in our personal relationships, the trivial obstacles that seem to fall across our paths, the sense of frustration with circumstances that don't support us. And yet suffering is optional, as a friend of mine has said. Not a day goes by when you're not at a choice point, a time when you can choose to stay in the context that is causing you pain or shift to one that is filled with possibility. We're all headed for the big nap. The real question isn't how good you are at overcoming the obstacles of life—the real question is, How good are you willing to have life be?

The redesigning of oneself I am talking about in this book does not come from grand visions—although grand visions may result. Instead, it's about the frame of mind you hold when you walk into a room. Whether your children, your fellow parents, or the board of directors are waiting for you there doesn't matter. The interplay of personalities, priorities, politics, and power in any group can be channeled or churned up depending on who you are being when you show up.

We assess right and wrong against the backdrop of experience or knowledge—the context that prevails in our culture and upbringing. Therein lies the challenge for all of us: to do things that violate the sacred rules of our logical minds. Habits are deep grooves in our lives, easy to trace and follow. Somewhere within us is a voice that informs us of another set of options, another life that is as ephemeral as a dream. What's counterintuitive is not necessarily illogical, but it can be difficult to see. And yet, it is freeing to break a habit, to innovate and create, because it places you outside a limiting context.

Change the way you think and your behavior will follow. Out of that comes changes to the world you will not be able to anticipate but that will support and affirm the instincts you're now expressing. In this book, you will go through the complicated, sometimes stressful, and emotionally provocative process of unearthing your fundamental beliefs about reality. Understanding that impact on your life and those around you gives you the opportunity to own your part in it all, even as you learn how to listen and be present for others. Getting in touch with your authentic self will help you trade up to a new context that expresses who you are while better serving the changes you seek in the world. You will also learn how to develop practices that keep your new expression whole until the mold is set and you gain a feeling of sturdiness and permanence about your self-designed way of being. You will soon see opportunities for engaging with others in new ways to new ends. It will no longer be about them or it, but about you in concert with those who matter most. Our concrete objective at the end of this book is for you to come up with your own groundbreaking project, expanding your influence to change your corner of the world in the way that you see fit.

My advice for getting the most value from this book is to read it thoroughly and in the order in which it lays out the five skills:

1. *Revealing* your existing contexts and putting each one in the form of a conclusion about your life. They should be brief enough to sound like a theme song title or a bumper sticker. For example, "If I always say yes people won't leave me."

2. *Take ownership* for each context as one that you have kept around for a long time. Assess its impediments and its virtues. It may be causing you problems, but it sure has helped you succeed too.

3. *Design* new contexts that will serve your best interests. Do this one at a time, and be sure that each new context is a frame of reference for living each day of your life. For example, "When I use my authentic voice, everyone ultimately benefits."

4. *Practice to sustain* your new context. Make a list of things to start and stop doing in order to build reliability for this new context.

5. *Engage* others in supporting your new context. Find people who will keep you honest about when you are operating from your new context and when you are backsliding into your old one.

We use the visual of a kaleidoscope (see Figure I.4) to represent the five trade-up skills. You know that when you turn the lens of a kaleidoscope only slightly, you see an entirely different image. It is the same with context shifting. Throughout this book and in your own daily practice, you will see that even the slightest adjustment in language can bring forth an entirely new way of being.

I believe all of us are on a journey of exploration. I also believe that all of us act as leaders when we seek to influence rather

Figure I.4   Kaleidoscope

than to react to the forces around us. A leader can transform an organization or a city park, a political group or a family, a team or a single self. By definition, a leader is someone who makes something happen on her shift. It starts when the pain point becomes too much and you say, "I must do this because. . . ." In order to get this work done, the leader must go beyond business as usual and generate radical and disruptive change through a community of like-minded true believers. You trade up from your old context to a new one in order to become the person who can make that transformation real.

Let's begin the journey!

1

IT'S ALL ABOUT YOU

Step 1. Reveal Your Prevailing Context

Leaders Create Fields of Influence
Awareness of my leadership presence and its impact on others
allows me to expand my influence and effectiveness.

Why REVEAL?

- Authentic expression
- Increased awareness
- Increased courage and vulnerability
- Enhanced community and partnership

Nothing in life is to be feared. It is only to be
understood.

—*Marie Curie*

Knowing others is intelligence; Knowing yourself is
true wisdom.
Mastering others is strength; Mastering yourself is
true power.

—*Tao Te Ching*

As a leader who aims to make a difference in the world, your most important job is to reveal and shift context, starting with your own. In this chapter, you will learn the fundamentals of revealing context (Step 1 in the five-step process) and gain an understanding of how to apply the practice of revealing and shifting contexts to your life. We'll go beyond an examination of your own factory-loaded operating system to explore how you can reveal and shift context in other individuals and even in organizations. As I mentioned in the Introduction, the people who come to me are either experiencing pain that is worth getting rid of or having a vision that is worth going for. That's what motivates them to break it all down and build it back up again.

The simplest way to think about revealing your context is to put all your beliefs about what is true in life on loudspeaker. Because our contexts are conclusions that exist for us as the truth, we don't question their validity. If I have a context that "I'm not good with numbers" I don't think of it as a context, I just operate from that belief system. It isn't until I say it out loud in front of someone else that I can be challenged as to its validity.

Your context is your presence, your belief system, your purpose. There is a set of behaviors that comes from that context as well as an impact produced by the overall system. *Revealing* is a process of looking inside to discover your unconscious beliefs and understand the interrelatedness of context, action, and impact.

Shifting is the act of changing or redesigning. When you shift context, you change your fundamental point of view about what is true. In other words, you trade your previous frame of reference for one that is more empowering or useful ... hence the phrase, "Trade up!"

Revealing and shifting context requires some heavy lifting (see Figure 1.1). It can be daunting and even anxiety inducing to consider moving the heavy boulders that cover the caves and tunnels that lead to your inner self. You may be reluctant to explore or expose

Figure 1.1   Reveal and Shift Context

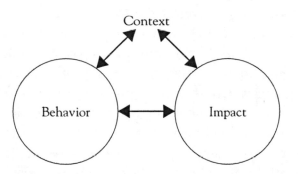

the fundamental beliefs you hold; and it can be painful, upsetting, or even flabbergasting to see how those views affect your life and those who share the world with you. The tools you gain in this book will make that heavy lifting easier—you'll acquire levers that you can learn to apply with increasing agility whenever those boulders get in your way.

Awareness of your automatic context is critical if you want to understand how people experience your personality and your leadership. We work on revealing context because it is the key to authentic self-expression; it helps us become more courageous about what we believe in and more open (and vulnerable) with others in the service of building relationships, partnerships, and community.

You may already be cognizant of what you care about and what has meaning for you—but few of us have the level of self-awareness necessary to perceive how we affect others. Because we are trapped in our own conclusions, we assume that everyone sees the world the same way we do, and we can't understand how reality can be interpreted so differently by other people. Is it any surprise that our relationships contain a string of unintended consequences?

Most people who make a genuine and well-intended attempt to change how they come across to others work on something simple and manageable, like their way of communicating. But while changes to the way you talk and listen help significantly, such changes are rarely sustainable. Beyond your words or facial expressions, it is your overall energy and your physical body that create the presence that impacts others at every moment. That energy derives out of your context—in other words, the "who you are being" in every encounter. As you will learn in this book, once you gain awareness of what your presence feels like to others, you can learn to modulate your power so that people receive you in a way that's helpful rather than hurtful, blocked, or misinterpreted. Once you learn to master that awareness by internalizing it, the practice of revealing and shifting context becomes your new default setting, allowing you to create positive change and forward progress in all of your relationships, whenever you choose.

Leadership and Horses

Prepare yourself for an idea that might seem strange or even bizarre, but that will help illustrate the point that your "personal energy"—"your way of being"—as directed by your context has a real physical impact on others. In this section of the chapter, you're going to see that a horse can not only lead you to water, it can even make you drink.

In my career, I have seen few methodologies for revealing context have as much impact as does the work of Ariana Strozzi-Heckler. Ariana, a pioneer in the field of equine education, created a body of work called "Leadership & Horses™," whose primary goal is to give people a fresh, innovative way to see how they are perceived as leaders. Before you start running out of the barn, let me provide some context on the history of horses and humans as "training buddies."

Humans and horses have worked together for a long time. In transportation, work, leisure, or entertainment, horses serve humans in exchange for food, shelter, and love. Horses don't care about a person's title or status, but they do insist on being led with a confident hand and they are inspired by clarity of purpose. As anyone who has tried to lead a horse knows, horses can act like enthusiastic performers or resentful employees. The response that a horse offers the person in the lead comes across as a highly visible form of feedback.

Ariana explains the connection best. As she puts it, leadership is not the sole purvey of human beings; "it exists throughout the animal kingdom as a practical way for social animals to communicate, negotiate, and collectively contribute to the survival of the individual and the whole." That fascinating observation tells us a lot about the reasons for leadership and the dynamics between those who lead and those who follow. Leadership is not a black-and-white case of command and control versus submit or resist; it is a subtle negotiation in the service of common goals, an interplay between the leader's vision and influence and the follower's level of commitment and contribution.

Horses, like humans, are natural belongers, intuitively sensitive to the dynamics of the group (or herd), ready and willing to make a contribution on behalf of anyone who demonstrates the capacity for providing clear direction. Because horses and humans have worked together for so many centuries, there is a special bond between us, one that helps amplify the sometimes invisible dynamics between leader and follower. As Ariana notes, the word *manage* comes from a Latin root meaning "to direct or train a horse." When a horse and human come together, the horse is super-sensitive to the relationship that gets established, focusing not on language—the strength of so many leaders—but on more subtle clues about how the leader is directing her energy, holding her body, and making her presence and intentions felt. As Ariana says, horses "listen to energy, intention, direction. They don't listen to stories." When the horse responds to the person holding the reins, it is not judging or criticizing the leader but rather evaluating the degree to which the person is in charge, the clarity of her goals, and the gap between what she says and what she is really communicating.

In a group setting, when I want to vividly demonstrate the very real influence a person's context has on her life, we spend some time at a ranch participating in equine-guided education. Each leader is asked to stand before the group of participants, hold the horse halter, and articulate what they are committed to as a leader. Then the leader proceeds to walk the horse around the corral, giving it three simple commands: walk, trot, and stop. What the leader will learn about herself in a 7- to 10-minute exercise will last a lifetime. Unlike humans, horses are not impressed by educational pedigree, financial wealth, or other common forms of stature. The horse is reading the leader's "way of being" and reacting to whether or not the leader is a strong, reliable leader who knows where she is going, will keep the horse safe if danger should arise, and will command respect throughout the duration of the exercise.

Even experienced horse lovers sometimes balk at this dubious proposition. What can horses teach us about our inner selves, let alone about our approach to leadership? And yet, everyone who has shared the experience with us expresses amazement at how clearly the horse provides feedback about the person leading it around the ring. It's one thing to have another person tell you that you are indecisive, pushy, frantic, passive, obsessively driven, dreamy, coldly pragmatic, or full of B.S. When a horse gives you the same message, in full view of witnesses, the truth is hard to ignore or repress. For many, it's the first epiphany on the road to a fundamental shift in being.

Some leaders can't get the horse to pick up the pace. Others can't get the horse to go in the direction they want. Some can metaphorically lead the horse to water, others can't make the horse drink. I've seen horses refuse to budge while the leader gets more and more flustered. I've seen horses race uncontrollably around the ring while the "leader" runs along behind. I've seen a horse listen to a leader's profound and meaningful statement of purpose and immediately poop, then do it again just as promptly the next time the leader speaks up. It's not a coincidence or an amazing feat of mass psychological transference—instead, the horse is surfacing and exposing the energy that everyone else feels in that leader's presence but can't consciously articulate. When you see how the horse reacts, you nod and think, "That's exactly how I feel, too, even though I didn't recognize it." For the leader, when the impact of her presence is revealed, that awareness can catalyze some deep and profound self-assessment. It can be uncomfortable at first, but it is immensely rewarding and worthwhile. It's the beginning of a journey, not an inquisition.

Learning how to reveal context is the critical step forward. Context influences everything. There is abundant scientific, sociological, and economic evidence that events (behaviors) and information (impact) change with changes in the environment (context). Children who are raised in loving environments have greater self-esteem, which tends to produce different behaviors and results than children raised in abusive environments. Companies that undergo reorganizations or major process redesigns like Total Quality Management or Six Sigma quickly revert to the old way of doing things if the environment or culture of the organization does not shift in context. Take an executive out of an organization, work on changing her, and put her back in the same organization, and the changes will fail to hold—or the executive will quit the organization. The same goes for a partner in a relationship. Without understanding the context we operate from, meaningful change doesn't have a chance.

When the people I work with become aware of their own contexts, the knowledge has a dramatic impact on their lives. You might think that top executives and high-energy entrepreneurs— women of significant education, great social standing, and tremendous accomplishment, successfully juggling partnerships, marriages, and children as well as careers, employees, and organizations— would be confident and clear of purpose all of the time. But every human being struggles with the same basic problem: each of us is trapped inside our own experiences, a condition that filters what we see and believe to be true and even possible. Complicating matters, the strengths that got us where we are today can severely hamper, blind, or block us going forward. It's not fair that we need to learn new skills and develop new strengths despite everything we've overcome or accomplished already. But it is within our capacity to do so, and it's up to us to make the effort when the outcomes really matter.

Work Hard, Be Nice

Sally Crawford is one of the leaders who experienced a revelation about her own context with Ariana Strozzi at the ranch. A highly successful chief executive officer, Sally has consistently put in hundred-hour weeks in building up a multimillion-dollar business she founded in her Chicago basement twenty-five years ago. Despite her forceful energy and passion, Sally does not resemble the stereotype of the hard-driven entrepreneur who demands the maximum from everyone around her. In fact, you couldn't meet a nicer, more articulate and caring person. She has a gentle sense of humor, great self-awareness, and empathy for others. Her high-tech consulting firm is one of the top women-owned businesses in Silicon Valley, serving a host of prestigious global clients. She has won awards and recognition, and she has taken on important leadership roles in helping other women in the technology field. What could be wrong with this picture?

In her unofficial biography, Sally says, "I have days when I long to bag groceries at Whole Foods, when the toughest decision I have to make is, paper or plastic?" When we met in our group, Sally admitted that in twenty years she hadn't taken off a single Thanksgiving holiday. Even in a room full of overachievers, this was a shock, and also a moment of guilty recognition. Everyone in an executive or leadership position knows that the demands of the job often go hand in hand with some kind of intense inner motivation, creating a leak among work, family, and me-time. Nevertheless, Sally's level of self-sacrifice was extreme.

Sally told us she had her wake-up call a few months before our gathering. She was working in her office over the Christmas holiday, clearing some paperwork away to get ready for the new year, when she discovered a yellowed note with a list of goals. Holding the note brought back a lot of memories. She'd made it a long time ago, only four years after founding her company. She'd always been a goal-oriented person. Looking at the list, she realized she had met all of the goals on the page except for the one that said,

"Work less hard." She couldn't help but sit there in amazement and wonder, "Why is this goal so elusive?"

The question brought with it some hard feelings. Her company had been extraordinarily successful. It had outlasted all its original peers. It had reinvented its business several times over, as was necessary in the high technology industry. Since 1982 they'd experienced two recessions, two market crashes, two wars, and four presidents. Despite it all, Crawford & Associates International had only downsized twice. In a near-superhuman exhibition of strength, resilience, and perseverance, Sally had put the company on her back repeatedly and had gotten everyone through the tough times and guided them through the good times. But after twenty years, she was coming to the realization that the effort wasn't sustainable anymore, for herself or for the organization. Sally was feeling something she'd never experienced during all those hundred-hour weeks and missed Thanksgivings: she was starting to feel resentful.

Sally understood that the impulse to do the heavy lifting and the hard pulling was deeply ingrained in her personality. "Like any type A person," she said, "you think you can do it by yourself. A leader has a helium-filled hand. It's always being raised into the air whenever something needs to be done." Unable to refuse a challenge or problem, Sally found her attitude was taking a toll. She was feeling, as she put it, like the jailer and the jailee—simultaneously in charge, but also imprisoned; the boss, but also the servant. Her days were a constant scramble to stay on top of everything that was going on, catch mistakes, help the business, and give others everything they needed to feel committed and happy. I've seen that approach and attitude toward leadership many times before, particularly among women leaders. Although Sally would never use these words, I call it being "the big Mother in the sky."

At Ariana's ranch, when Sally had her turn with the horse, the "presence" she brought to work became readily apparent. Weighing less than 100 pounds, Sally seemed tiny next to the huge beast. Holding it by the reins, she couldn't get it to move, so she started stroking it, touching it, petting it, all while saying pleasant things to it. To those of us watching, the message was clear. Sally wasn't able to lead the horse around the ring, so she put all of her emotional energy into being nice to it.

No dummy, Sally immediately understood the significance of this approach. It was such a clear analogy to what she did at her organization, it wasn't even funny. Over the ensuing days, she began to create more clarity around that epiphany. She realized that "carrying people" was something she *did*, not something she was *forced* to do. Most of her people were extremely hard working and extremely nice—just like her. But the organization paid a price for this. Sally was willing, for example, to employ some people who were not pulling their own weight. It wasn't their fault; it was hers. They were good people, but they weren't suited for the job. She was hanging on to them too long, or failing to encourage or empower them in ways that would allow them to carry more of the load. Instead of letting them go, Sally put all of her energy into making payroll to keep the organization's roof over everyone's head. It was not good for the organization, and it was certainly not good for Sally. Even more enlightening, Sally realized that her "carrying people" approach was not good for those she was helping along. There's an expression in the horse world: "leading a horse straight to the glue factory." It's a brutal acknowledgment that horses are working animals with upkeep that's too costly to justify if the horse is not pulling its weight. If you fail to give a horse a meaningful job—whether that's winning the Kentucky Derby or pulling a plow—you're not doing the horse any favor; instead, you're leading it to the glue factory. Sally was doing the same thing with some of her people, and that realization hit her hard. Sally ended up reorganizing the company in a way that relieved those burdens. It was not easy to let people go, but it was the right thing to do for the business.

Over the ensuing days of the program, Sally worked hard to put all of these revelations into words. She came to understand her default context: "In order to survive I must work extremely hard and be extremely nice." Once articulated, it wasn't difficult for her to figure out where that context came from. She's a twin but was never the equal. As the smaller, more sickly, and unexpected child, she had to fight hard to be healthy, and then she had to keep fighting as she grew up. For example, her sister was a naturally gifted student who got all A's throughout school. Sally got C's until she kicked into gear and worked harder, obtaining straight A's in college except for a single B. As for being extremely nice, her home life growing up was no bed of roses. She was always the peacemaker, the conciliator, the one making things better for everyone else. She learned strategies for helping people get along while avoiding conflict.

Was there anything so wrong with Sally's approach to life? In fact, working hard and being nice had served her extremely well and gotten her far; it was a terrific way of dealing with the world, filled with optimism and kindness, that had enriched her personally while helping others as well. She'd accomplished a lot, made a difference in many people's lives, and her company was very successful. But by the time she saw the list of goals from twenty years before and read the unchecked item, "Work less hard," she knew inside that her approach was no longer sustainable. Being indispensable to others gets old after twenty or more years. She'd been there and done that, and she wanted a change while still remaining committed to her organization and her people.

To shift her context, Sally tried to think about work in a different way, hoping to prove to herself that it didn't always have to be so hard. She wanted to enjoy her days more and have more space in them. Her initial changes in that regard were simple but very effective. She resolved to begin each day with a hike and end each day with yoga. She'd been practicing yoga for thirteen years, but she still found it difficult to be "present" while holding a pose rather than thinking about a hundred other things. That multitasking mind-set was symptomatic of the way she operated in general, always doing more than one thing at once, checking e-mails while talking on the cell phone, going over papers while riding in the back of a taxi. She made a deliberate effort going forward to center herself and be in the moment, practicing the art of giving her full attention to the person or task in front of her.

Sally knew that any personal change she made could not take place in a vacuum. As the leader of her company, she'd created a culture of people who were also very hard working and very nice. Because they were in the consulting business, it was easy to bend over backward for every client, take on more than was humanly possible, overpromise and then work like the devil to deliver on those promises while exceeding expectations. Her organization, in order to be sustainable, needed to develop a sense of self-respect and self-appreciation that would allow each person working there to set boundaries and avoid going overboard with clients all the time. In other words, everyone in her company had to learn to shift context, too. They needed to understand that a day doesn't have to be totally filled up—that it's okay to have some white space in life, that you can still feel satisfied when work is not brutal, taxing, and exhausting.

The shift was a challenge for all involved. The work-hard-be-nice context was incredibly ingrained in Sally and her organization. She was used to relying on that approach to get through tough projects. She realized that she needed to replace her old context with one that was equally compelling and useful. That's when she understood she didn't yet have a clear vision about what she wanted to accomplish, and the lack of that vision was an obstacle going forward. She came back to us for more work, focusing on learning the power of holding a clear vision. This time, standing with the horse, she became very present and mindful of what she wanted to do. Clicking twice, she began walking forward, reins in hand. The horse stayed with her shoulder to shoulder all the way around the corral. It was a remarkable change from her previous experience, one that confirmed how important it was for her to work on being deliberate and clear of purpose.

The Power of Shifting Others' Contexts

Sally formulated her new vision and brought it back to work. As a leader, she would now be extremely focused on building organizational capability—in terms of systems, people, processes, and strategy—in order to make the organization more sustainable. In order to accomplish that vision—as she learned with the horse—she would need to be clear in her direction at all times. Sally had an old habit of openly waffling and debating decisions, bringing a wide array of people into the leadership conversation. Going forward, she worked diligently to be more mindful and focused about her vision and direction in every interaction, presenting her employees with clear leadership decisions. She noticed her people relaxing as a result and saw that they required less hand-holding and cajoling. It was tangible evidence that supported her new context and helped make those efforts more sustainable for everyone in turn.

Soon, an opportunity to solidify the break with old patterns and exert new leadership arose. Sally's team was working with a client on a big project. On the client's side, there were two leaders in charge, creating a series of crossed signals and lost time. Eventually, after one of the leaders left, the way forward seemed easier. Sally was elated. "Finally," she thought, "we've got clear line of sight and clear direction. It's time to knock this one out of the park." But when she checked in with her team, she found them devastated. They were stuck on the fact that they only had two weeks left to do the work.

If Sally had not undergone her training in context shifting, she might have pushed and pulled, petted and cheered her people to no effect, before doing the brunt of the work herself. Instead, she was able to recognize the context the group was operating in—a collective belief that the situation was hopeless, without enough time to pull a winning solution together—and concentrate on changing that view. She focused on her team leader first, a young woman with tremendous leadership potential. Sally helped the team leader look at the situation in a different way. The young woman came to view the circumstances not as a hopeless and imminent failure, but as an opportunity to rally her own team. In turn, the team leader helped the other members of the team understand that their belief the project was hopeless was not a prophesy written in stone, but a preformed conclusion limiting their chances for success.

To complicate matters, the deadline fell on the Tuesday after a holiday weekend. Everyone wanted to be home with their families. The team leader rallied the team and got them to see that it was possible and worthwhile to accomplish their goal, while acknowledging openly that it was just as important to meet family and holiday obligations. They would each take turns at home, in accordance with their individual situations, coming up with a balance or trade-off that everyone felt comfortable with. For her part, Sally stayed in the background, resisting the instinct to jump in, knowing it was important to be present but to not be the one pulling the load. She took the opportunity to be a role model more than a leader, using humor to improve everyone's spirits, and taking her own time off that Friday to bake cupcakes for her children. Likewise, everyone else managed to fit in family time with work time too.

In the end, the project was such a tremendous success that the client organization gave the team a standing ovation. Just as important, the team saw that family time was valued, even during a crisis, and that getting through a tough assignment could be enjoyable rather than exhausting and draining. It was an episode that showed a culture change was taking hold, and everyone was achieving a more sustainable way of working.

Shifting Team Contexts

Let me give you two examples of how this can happen in a team environment. I was a professional softball player. When my daughter was seven, I was asked to coach her Peppermint Patty team. If you've ever seen seven-year-old girls engaging in competitive team sports for the first time, you can imagine the challenge I was in for. We started off slowly, doing drills and exercises, practicing fly balls and grounders. By the third day, I was ready to teach them how to bat. I lined up each girl at home plate, showed them the proper stance, got them to hold the bat on the shoulder, and taught them how to swing. Then I told the girls that I was going to toss a soft squishy ball lightly toward the plate, and asked them to hit the ball with the bat when it got close.

The first girl was ready. I gave the ball a baby toss from 8 feet away. When the ball neared the girl she screeched and ducked. I didn't want to scare her, so we went on to the next girl. I gave the ball a gentle baby toss. The second girl screeched and ducked. I knew then it was going to be a long practice.

Obviously, nothing I could say or teach them about holding the bat or keeping their eye on the ball would produce nicely hit singles. Being in the context-shifting business, however, I knew that focusing on behaviors or impact was not the answer. I had to step back and change their context first.

To me, that context was clear. An object tossed their way was something to be feared, more like a bullet than like a ball. So I went to the trunk of my car and retrieved a package of whiteboard markers. Then, I drew a different color smiley face on each panel of the soft squishy baseball. When I was done, I told the girls that we were going to stop playing "hit the ball." This time, I wanted them to stand in the box without the bat and name the color of the smiley face that went by when the ball passed them. The first girl stood at the ready, I tossed the ball, and she called out, "Blue!" This was a lot more fun. Each girl got into line for her turn, squealing out the colors. Next, I asked them to try the game again, but this time with the bat on their shoulder. Again, they were able to yell out the colors as the ball went by. Finally, on our last turn, I asked them to continue to watch for the color of the smiley face but also reach out with the bat and touch the ball as it went by.

Over and over, the tossed balls came back to me, hit by the bat. We played our first game the following Tuesday, and beat the other team 29–0. As a leader, the only thing I did was shift the girls' context from baseball as speeding bullet to baseball as floating beach ball.

I had a similar experience in the business world working with a Gillette subsidiary in Belmont, California. Between 1997 and 2000, nearly forty women in the Oral-B Laboratories participated in our Women Leading Change program. At that time, Oral-B was experimenting with rapid new product development processes and dedicated project teams. Using the leadership skill of context shifting, those forty women led the development of the CrossAction toothbrush.

The CrossAction toothbrush was an outstanding example of breakthrough in product design, development, and manufacturing; clinical methods development; claim support results; consumer evaluation methods; and common effort in cross-functional teaming. The product has been successful in the marketplace and has won numerous design and packaging awards. The breakthrough was based on the questioning of a simple conclusion. It was always thought that toothbrush bristles had to go straight up and down to remove plaque. As a result, every company in the industry produced toothbrushes that only gained incremental improvement, decade after decade. The CrossAction toothbrush not only revolutionized plaque removal but surfaced additional limiting conclusions about dental floss, mouthwash, and even how to develop a mentoring program managed by employees.

Once you pull the string of the most secure conclusions you hold, you will be amazed at what gets revealed.

Not Smart-Pretty-Good Enough

Jeanie Bunker is another example of someone with an incredible track record of success and accomplishment but marred for a long time by secret feelings of inadequacy. From the outside, you would never imagine any insecurity. Jeanie is a force of nature. She's held top executive jobs at E*Trade and Yahoo. She talks quickly and with an intelligence and energy that can be exhausting, as though life in her orbit is a constant whirlwind of activity. We first met when she attended a short workshop I gave called "Leading Through Influence." Jeanie was a clear mover and shaker among the attendees, a status that stood out to everyone but her.

Jeanie had signed up because she'd reached a level in the hierarchy of her global organization where she was working with many business leaders from across functions but was uncertain how to manage people she had no formal authority over. Jeanie was in charge of the marketing budget during the planning cycle and her job was to decide which general manager (GM) got what in terms of marketing resources. As you can imagine this was not a conflict- or stress-free position to be in. While Jeanie needed to consider marketing from a strategic organizational perspective, every GM pushed hard for her own needs.

"It was a messy communication process," Jeanie recalls. "People were trying to push and threaten me into doing things, and I felt like I was not in control, and not strong enough to stand up to everybody. I was losing my balance. I was completely exhausted." Complicating matters, she got no support from senior management, who were just as lost in terms of figuring out how to deal with the complexity of managing resources in a booming organization. But Jeanie applied the salt in the wound herself. She hadn't had the time to position herself strategically within her own group to share the workload with her direct reports. As a result, she ended up doing all the heavy lifting alone. "I was meeting for nine to ten hours a day. Every hour was booked with someone who had a heated, high-pressure, urgent need."

In our workshop, Jeanie picked up some helpful tips and tools. Most important, she learned the strategy of listening carefully to the concerns of her business partners. "I was coming to them overloaded with my problems, and telling them what to do." Rather than alleviating the stressful circumstances, Jeanie was feeding the fire. We helped Jeanie learn to slow down and make the effort to determine where her own concerns and her business partners' concerns overlapped, as a way of finding a connection in terms of commitment and passion.

Jeanie recalls how well this strategy worked with one GM. Before the influencing workshop, Jan, who was a close friend of Jeanie's, met with Jeanie to demand additional resources from the central budget pool. Jeanie had to deny the request because Jan's business was not a strategic priority of the firm. The interaction was heated and both women were under intense pressure. Jan left the meeting feeling, according to Jeanie, "like I had dumped on her, and wrecked her business." After the influencing workshop, Jeanie called Jan to talk again about the situation. This time, Jeanie explained the strategic priorities of the firm and promised that if she had any money left over once those needs were met, Jan could have her request. Jan's reaction was completely different from before. She felt included in the conversation, and she was impressed by the amount of money the firm was investing in its vision. She left feeling that she could support Jeanie because she knew there was a solid rationale behind the decision-making process. Two years later, when Jan was heading a new strategic business, she showed up in Jeanie's office again. Their relationship was on great terms, and they had an exciting discussion of how Jeanie could support Jan's venture with resources.

Through an important change in Jeanie's behavior, she had achieved a much better outcome. This was a good thing, but ironically, Jeanie's new success at partnering boosted her reputation and got her a fast promotion to vice president with additional responsibilities. Even though she was now a better communicator, she still felt out of control. Her energy output was like a fire hose she could barely hang on to.

Weary from the unrelenting stress of her job and curious about the possibilities of context shifting, Jeanie came back for some deeper work. Used to a frenzy of activity, she found the slow pace of the apparently agenda-less first day almost impossible to stand. Yet the role plays and the exchange of stories with other executives triggered powerful emotions within her. At night, she was unable to sleep, her brain racing, wondering, "Why do I operate the way I operate? Where does it come from? Why am I being insecure in this workshop? What's going on?"

Jeanie understood that each activity of the day had placed her in a stressful situation that stimulated her fight-or-flight response. The high-energy version of her that kept showing up in the room as a result wasn't out of character, it was the deepest part of her, put on loudspeaker for everyone to hear. When she worked with the horses later that day, Jeanie saw her presence amplified again.

While the horse didn't move for some people, it raced around the corral for Jeanie. There was no control or direction, just boundless activity, feeding off Jeanie's own barely containable energy.

Soon, she began to put words to the revelations. "I found out I am a doer," she said. "I have that 'I get shit done' mentality." The problem was that she couldn't modulate her energy level. "It was scary. For somebody who is supposed to be leading a team, it was amazing how much stuff I was doing. After the influencing workshop, I was having better quality conversations, but I was still having hundreds of them, micromanaging everywhere, taking care of everybody."

During the context-shifting workshop, Jeanie started to "excavate her brain," as she put it. "I started to uncover subconscious things that drive me and make me behave the way I do. I realized that while I always think I am choosing how to act, I'm actually on autopilot. Add a little stress to my day, and whatever is habit shows up." Those habits were taking their toll, Jeanie noted in describing her life. "You do not exercise, you do not get adrenalin reduction, you do not get oxygen. You go home late and everybody is mad at you. You go to bed and wake up at 4 A.M. because there are three e-mails you should have sent. The brain of an executive women is on such hyperdrive that there is no rest, and no chance to reengage."

Everywhere Jeanie looked, she saw examples of how her way of being was influencing her life. It felt as though she was standing in a hall of mirrors, staring at her own face at every compass point, unable to find a way out. But once she contemplated her own behaviors, Jeanie recognized where they came from and was quickly able to put words to them. "I started to hear myself," she said. "I'm one of five children, I'm learning disabled, and I have an insatiable critic as a father and an alcoholic narcissistic mom. What did I come out of that with? The understanding that I am not smart enough, not pretty enough, and not good enough at anything."

Naturally, Jeanie has always been relentlessly driven. Despite her perceived limitations, she obtained a Masters in International Finance from Georgetown University. In her career, each job she's taken has been an upgrade in responsibility and power. Along the way, her father criticized her career moves as dead ends and wastes of time. When she entered a new firm with twice the pay and responsibility, he questioned the move because her title was below the one she'd held at her previous firm. When she quickly made senior vice president, he said, "I guess you were going to catch up at some point." It never ceases to amaze me how much impact a parent's approval can continue to have over a child well into maturity.

In our workshop, Jeanie began to peel back the layers. Like the other executives, she had introduced herself with her happy story—the position of power and accomplishment, the loving relationship, the two wonderful children. But after doing some work on revealing context, she was able to tell the real story. "I'm freaking out," she said. "I feel out of control. My family is angry at me because I'm never around, and I'm doing the work for the money." Her long-standing context had gotten her far, but at what cost? She was always trying to be smarter, more collected, the one with all the answers. It didn't feel good, it wasn't healthy, and it wasn't serving her family or her life the way she wanted.

Jeanie knew she wanted to change, and very quickly an objective came to mind. Even though overpowering energy had always defined her life, she'd also been blessed with an amazing knack for having good things happen magically. It was a quality she recognized in her son. "We call him serendipity boy. He shows up somewhere and has an expectation that something is going to happen—and it happens. And I've realized I have the same thing. It's this sense of connecting all the dots magically, and seeing things converge at the right time and place. That's another thing people like about me and why they like to work with me—I can ask a few questions and we come up with the magical nonlinear solution." She wanted to learn how to draw on that positive capability more deliberately. It became her new context—a trade-up from "Not good enough and never going to get there" to "I bring magic and passion to make dreams come true."

How to get there? She knew she needed to do less and become more strategic about her efforts in order to give herself the time to float and think. Accomplishing that required getting her partner, her family, and—most important—her administrative assistant aligned to her new goal. She asked her admin for help in not allowing her to overschedule her day. She blocked out time for hikes before work and for thinking during the morning. She no longer scheduled meetings after five. Her admin was in shock, since Jeanie typically scheduled every hour of the week, but she also loved being able to play a strategic role on Jeanie's behalf and helped Jeanie be more efficient about preparing for meetings. Her partner helped Jeanie stick to her new goals, establishing an expectation that Jeanie would now be home at a reasonable hour. Jeanie slowed down. She stopped checking e-mails on Saturdays and took Sundays off. She allowed the serendipity to seep into her life.

Leading the Next Context Shift

Revealing context is only the first stage in a larger game—in a way, it's the point at which the work begins. For instance, despite her best efforts and the strong support of those around her, Jeanie began to find it hard to keep her new context going. Within a few months, she had doubts as to whether "creating magic" was the right metaphor for her life, and she continued to have trouble modulating her energy. Sometimes it was working, on other days she felt very disconnected. Eventually, she realized that she was doing the work of context shifting solely in her brain. She needed to go deeper still, and focus on rooting those changes in her physical body in order to help them take hold. We talk about that kind of work in later chapters.

This work is important for anyone, but it is especially critical for leaders. I define *leadership* as the ability to speak, listen, and evoke action on behalf of a compelling future. Leadership, by its very nature, has change as its goal, whether that change is focused on the individual, the organization, or the community. There's no need for anyone to lead if your group remains headed in the same direction at the same speed. Real leadership gets called upon when you are moving from a state or condition that is no longer acceptable to a future that is new, exciting, and necessary.

As a leader, your job is to illuminate all the conscious or unconscious beliefs, myths, assumptions, and preconceptions that form your own conclusions and the conclusions of the people around you. From there, your job is to jettison conclusions that are limiting, and see that new contexts take root that will allow you and your group, organization, or community to grow. Your ability to see and invent conclusions that empower yourself, your team, or your organization determines what kind of future becomes available. If that ability is limited, it will limit the scope of what can be achieved, putting a lid on the creativity, energy, and enthusiasm of others. When that ability has been honed and exercised, it can be inspiring in ways even the leader can't anticipate.

What's going to happen on your shift? You are 100 percent responsible no matter what. It is up to you to master the art of revealing and shifting context, starting with your own.

Putting It into Words: Cracking the Code

Nothing about Sally Crawford's work-hard-be-nice context surprised her, and yet she'd never put it into words before; as a result, she'd never thought about it consciously. Once she revealed and articulated that context, she was amazed to realize how great a hold it had over her life. I've seen this kind of revelation again and again. We think we are rational beings, more or less in control of the way we come across. But in the ruckus of the day to day, we don't recognize that our attitudes and responses to events and people are based largely on the deeply ingrained way we see the world. If we search for the source of that belief system, we notice how consistently the strata run over time, often all the way to childhood, formed by the emotional pressures of our families and early experiences.

Revealing Context Is All in the Language You Use

To articulate Sally's context, she first put it into words. The secret to effectively revealing your context is to capture it in the form it typically occurs in your head. In other words, simplify it into a one-sentence motto that describes how you operate on a daily basis. Here's how you can do this for yourself. A contextual phrase often has an "expression" and a "tail." The expression is that aspect of the truth that you are more willing to say out loud. The tail points to the feeling or impression you unwittingly leave other people with—the unintended impact you have. A "bridge word" combines your context to its tail in such a way that it helps you understand the connection between how you are being and how you impact others. Use Table 1.1 to explore versions of your prevailing context. Know that it might not be pretty! Not every default context follows this format, but it's a good place to start.

Examples:

I am self-sufficient . . . *because* (I don't trust people).

I have high standards . . . *therefore* (I am better than you).

I am a master problem solver . . . *so* (you will need me to get anything done).

Table 1.1 Context, Bridge Word, and Tail

Context	Bridge Word	Tail
_____	but	_____
_____	so	_____
_____	and	_____
_____	because	_____
_____	in order to	_____
_____	therefore	_____

Although this can look simple on paper, getting to the essence of your contextual expression and its tail can be a challenge. Before your context gets articulated, it remains abstract and elusive, a force you don't even really know exists. I suggest, therefore, that you think about your context as a kind of genetic code that can be cracked by identifying its components. Rather than a double helix and strands of intertwined molecules, the context code is based on a dynamic system of three dimensions: (1) your presence, or "who you be" with others, which produces (2) your actions and (3) your impact. Figures 1.2 and 1.3 illustrate this.

We can see signs or evidence of your context by looking at the two circles of actions and impact in Figure 1.3. For example, sometimes the impact we have on others is desirable, and other times we produce unintended impact. There are times when I want to impact my daughter by convincing her to get her homework done in advance of the deadline. Obviously I am a conscientious parent and hope to instill a good educational work ethic in her. Instead it is often the case that I produce annoyance and withdrawal from her. While that was not my intention, it was still a clear impact that I produced. I like to say that "if it's happening on your shift, then you've got something to do with it!"

Impact arises from action, which is represented by the left-hand circle. Action can take the form of behaviors, activities,

Figure 1.2 Presence

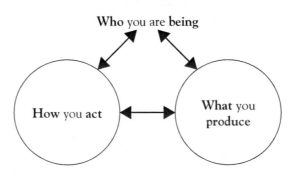

Figure 1.3   The DNA of Context Shifting

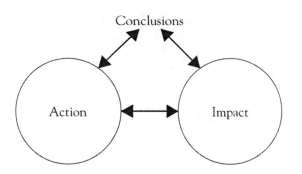

speaking, listening, and so on. In the example with my daughter, my actions were twofold. I said, "Chelsea, since you have some free time you should get your term paper done before it is due on Tuesday." Additionally, I rested my hands on my hips as I was talking and smiling. Seems pretty straightforward and well intentioned, right? Unfortunately I wasn't successful in producing the impact that I wanted. She barked at me to let her run her own life and promptly shut her bedroom door.

This unintended outcome can be explained via the third part of the figure: conclusions. Remember my context shift in the Introduction? My original context was centered in hard work and 100 percent application to achieve goals, and this point of view was like a physical force getting in the way of my best intentions with Chelsea.

"I'll never get anywhere in life without my nose to the grindstone" was a deeply embedded conclusion I'd chosen to believe in (see Figure 1.4). In my world, that meant if you didn't work hard on your term paper, you didn't get anywhere. It wasn't until I was able to surface that context that I could see that not everyone shared my view of reality. My desire to shift out of that context arose because I was unhappy with the impact my actions were causing in my life and in the lives of people around me.

Now, let's look at how a trade-up in context affected my behavior and impact. When I came up with the conclusion,

Figure 1.4   Nose to the Grindstone

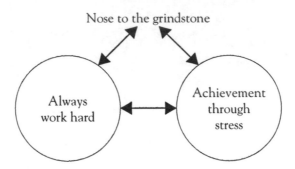

"It all turns out with grace and ease," I recognized an environment my body and spirit could settle into (see Figure 1.5). That doesn't mean it was easy to develop my new behaviors. I needed to rely on the discipline of practice, the support of others, and an openness to feedback in order to make it. But having established the right environment or context for my new behaviors, I was able to help them grow and ultimately flourish.

Sally Crawford's context shift redesigned her life and organization. When she traded up from "work hard, be nice" to a context that supported her desire for more sustainable leadership, she created an environment in which new behaviors could take root.

Most people, when they try to undergo personal change, focus solely on impact or action because these are more concrete manifestations of context. In my work, we go backward from

Figure 1.5   It All Turns Out with Grace and Ease

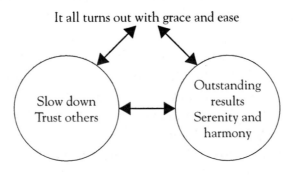

impact and action to change context, because then we can transform the entire system.

For the Sake of What?

Why should you want to change your context? We all need a
motivation for engaging in deep personal work. I ask each person, "For the sake of what do you reveal?" I'm looking to create
the stirrings of a vision, to unearth the passion that is too often
buried beneath a lifetime of dead-end conclusions. Analyzing
your context just to understand it would not be an empty exercise, but if you lacked significant motivation or a compelling
desire to change, I doubt whether you would have the time,
energy, or focus necessary to dig deep and stay the course. Most
people are motivated because there is some compelling future
they want to achieve or some point of pain they want to relieve.
The more insistent those needs are, the more likely it is the person will follow through.

What context are you operating from? It's difficult to determine without knowing how to follow the right clues. The impe-
tus for beginning your investigation usually arises out of your
behavior or the impact you have in the world. If you don't see
the behavior or impact you want, then you work backward from
there to change your context, because then you can change
everything. You may be concerned about an undesired or unintended impact, or you may be pursuing a desired impact. For
example, you may wish to improve a stale relationship with your
spouse, or you may envision your marketing team doubling its
numbers. In either case, the desire for a different impact drives
your efforts at context shifting. Likewise, you can begin your
quest because you are motivated by the need to change an undesirable behavior or the need to put in place a behavior you want
to include in your personal arsenal. You may wish, for example,
that you didn't always frustrate your son, or you may wish that
you could be a more passionate public speaker. The desire for a

different behavior will lead to the source of that behavior: the context from which you are operating.

Giving an authentic voice to that context is critical. We have a tendency, especially when we're talking out loud, to neutralize a context statement by talking about it in the third person or in a way that downplays the emotional impact. For example, one woman I worked with described her context as being one of low self-esteem. I knew, from having listened to her talk about her life, that "low self-esteem" didn't quite cut it. When she came back, later that day, with a new way of articulating her context, the statement really hit home. "I'm a piece of crap," she said. We both understood that the wrenching power of that statement was rooted in its honesty and echoed the way her default setting sounded in her own head all of the time. "I'm a piece of crap" was the reality she lived with every day, the conclusions that served as her operating system in just about every interaction. Articulating it so harshly gave her access to a deep and difficult understanding about her upbringing and relationships; and it helped immeasurably in her motivation to trade up to something worthy of her and the gifts she regularly brings to the world.

Context is a constant connection between "being" and "truth," or who you are, how you come across, and what reality surrounds you. Understanding context requires great perception and vigilant self-awareness. Creating a new context can be rife with challenges. You can't easily divorce what you believe from how you want it to be. But we are language animals, and we can analyze, break down, and rebuild our contexts through metaphor. We are also social animals, and it should not be forgotten that building a new context needs to be done in the company of those who love and support us (see Figure 1.6).

What's below the surface of your complex life? Revealing answers the question, What is shaping or limiting who you are, what you do, and how you learn? That examination can take place at the individual level or in an organization of many thousands of people. What emerges from such an investigation is the choice to achieve new purpose, a new self-awareness about how

Figure 1.6   Developing a New Presence

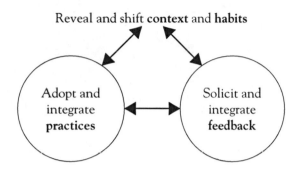

Reveal and shift **context** and **habits**

Adopt and integrate **practices**

Solicit and integrate **feedback**

you operate and why. If it were possible to fundamentally shift your context, what opportunities would become available? Why do those opportunities matter to you? What different results could you, your team, or your organization produce? Our automatic responses to life are based on the system that we are firmly embedded in. We can choose a different reaction once that pattern is revealed.

Taking the Step

When revealing your context, remember to put it in the form of a conclusion—for example, "If I show them how smart I am they will include me in their circle." Sometimes it is easier to start from an undesirable situation and work backward to reveal your context. For instance, if you were passed over for promotion and this is a recurring theme, then you may begin to see a pattern or context reaching all the way back to grade school: for example, "Even when I give it my best, I never get rewarded." The main instruction for revealing is to experiment with different phrases until you reach an *Aha!* moment of recognition. You can use Figure 1.7 to map out your context. It is not as important that you get it exactly right as it is that you recognize the familiarity of the words and feelings.

Figure 1.7   Map Out How Your Context Works

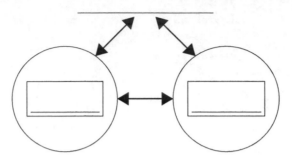

It's exciting to uncover our unconscious beliefs and conclusions and begin to rework them. Oftentimes, though, people want to jump from Reveal (Step 1) to Design (Step 3) without immersing themselves in Step 2: the critical step of owning their context. Let's find out why owning is the essential gatekeeper to real transformative change.

2

FROM BUG SOUP TO BUTTERFLY

Step 2. Own Your Context

Take Responsibility for Your Context and Be Accountable for Changing It
The willingness to accept my prevailing context with both its upside and downside gives me the freedom to choose a more powerful context.

Why OWN?

- Freedom of choice
- Advancement of commitments and concerns
- Increased connection

The last of the human freedoms—to choose one's attitude in any given set of circumstances, to choose one's own way.

—*Victor Frankl*

There is a vitality, a life force, an energy, a
quickening that is translated into action, and
because there is only one of you in all of time, this
expression is unique. And if you block it, it will
never exist. . . . It is not your business to determine
how good it is, nor how it compares with other
expressions. It is your business to keep the channel
open.

—*Martha Graham*

Your willingness to acknowledge and accept the existence of
your prevailing context (even though it might cause you pain,
shame, frustration, or anxiety) gives you the freedom to choose a
more powerful context. That doesn't mean such freedom will feel
exciting or even good at this stage in your journey. I'm reminded
of an old Garfield cartoon. Sneaking into a pet store, Garfield runs
through the aisles opening the cage doors and calling out to the
animals, "You're free! You're free!" When he realizes none of
the animals are seizing the opportunity to escape, he looks back
and sees the frightened and anxious looks on their faces. So Garfield runs through the pet store again, this time closing all the cage
doors, yelling, "You're safe! You're safe!"

Your old context may not have always provided the best
approach or attitude for the life you want to lead, but it had its
upside. It was comfortable and safe, and it gave you the sanctuary
of profound certainty whenever you felt threatened, anxious, or
stressed. Naturally, your attachment to the context of the past
underscores the ease with which you can drift back into old habits
or ways of thinking if you are not deliberate about reinforcing your
changes. Think of how difficult it is to break away from bad eat-
ing habits ("I can have a few cookies for dessert because I skipped
lunch") or an addiction ("One drink won't hurt me"), and you
can appreciate how difficult it can be to break away from a mind-
set that's been reinforced over a lifetime and is as comfortable as
an old shoe.

It would be wonderful, once we finally acknowledged the limitations of our old context, if our spirit responded to the new freedom with boundless energy and optimism. Unfortunately, that is not the case, or, more accurately, any energy and optimism we feel can be difficult to sustain through the hard work of getting a new context up and running.

In fact, the first step of context shifting—Reveal—is a step that often leaves people in despair. Any positive emotions are easily overwhelmed by sometimes deep and wrenching feelings. You might feel shaken up, as though your world has been turned upside down. You might feel angry about the cage you've been in for so long and blame others—*those parents again!*—for the prevailing context you inherited. You might feel shame or guilt about the impact your context has had on the people closest to you. And you might feel uncertain about whether you have the capacity to do anything different and better, or you may feel lost about where to go next. As I emphasize later in this book, it's important that you avoid dealing with all of these emotions solo. *Your head is like a bad neighborhood. Don't go in there alone!*

You can be comforted in knowing that all of those difficult feelings are natural and that everyone is susceptible to them. They are also dangerous, because as human beings we are prone to make quick retreats to whatever has provided us shelter in the past, no matter how limiting or detrimental.

In this chapter we look closely at the signs you will notice and the pitfalls that await you while you exist between contexts. We'll acknowledge and even celebrate what your old context has done for you and give it a proper burial. And we'll start to get excited about the new possibilities around the corner.

The Context Audit

Once your context has been revealed in Step 1, the most important thing is to "own" it before moving on. Unfortunately, the idea of owning the context you currently operate in is also a bit of a paradox. How can you own something you inherited, that may even feel as though it had been forced upon you? Your context is a mishmash of overwhelming influences. You've got your parents, and their parents, some of your relatives and teachers, the other kids you grew up around, the culture you were surrounded by, including whatever church, community, school, or political system you found yourself immersed in, not to mention the tenor of the times. In fact, some of those contextual influences may feel like Darwin's evolutionary curse, the DNA that holds a grip on humanity itself. (Unless, of course, you don't believe in evolution, which only means you've got another context to deal with.)

So the good news: hey, it's not your fault! That context you've been operating within for thirty, forty, fifty, or sixty years . . . you didn't create it, you just got stuck with it. On the other hand, by this point in your life, do you have any doubt that you're 100 percent responsible for your context? In perpetuating a context, we all do a dance between adoption and volition, a jig we're pretty good at by the time we've hit our stride in life. Revealing your context also helps you understand the many times and ways you've actively embraced that context during your life, allowing it to be your willing partner. I bet that, looking back over key incidents, you can track, in many nuanced moments, how you perpetuated that context, nurtured it, caused it to flourish, forced its will onto others, and probably passed it on to your own children like a treasured family heirloom.

Enough with the guilt. There was nothing wrong or bad about what you did. In taking ownership for your context you are not setting yourself up for blame or fault. Acknowledging that you've been operating in a certain way for a long time is not an indictment of your character. In fact, the reason you chose to run with your prevailing context for so long is that it gave you all kinds of wonderful goodies.

Always Seek Candid and Timely Feedback

Let's talk a bit about the concept of feedback. Most people, when they hear the word *feedback*, think about its negative connotations.

If someone in the office says, "I have some feedback for you," you brace yourself for a harangue that will undoubtedly make you feel bad rather than good. On the other hand, there's lots of feedback we get in life all the time that actually feels very good—we just don't call it feedback. When you stay late at the office every evening, finish your project ahead of schedule, and get an unexpected promotion—that's feedback. Chances are, you'll continue your late-evening ways in your new position because those efforts have been supported and reinforced by positive outcomes in the past. Heck, you may even come to believe that good things only happen by working late. On the other hand, if you rarely put in the hours, rely on your wit and charm to wow them in the meeting, and manage to get the promotion anyway, that's feedback, too—feedback that's telling you to relax, take it easy, and don't work, just dazzle them with your smile.

The goodies you get from your prevailing context do a powerful job of making you feel right. In fact, if your context didn't have a significant upside, it wouldn't last. My context—"nose to the grindstone"—sure gave me a lot of goodies. I don't even have to think hard to add them all up. I was rewarded with praise, trophies, and good grades growing up and was able to move on from my modest upbringing to much bigger and more exciting pastures. I was a wild success in college and I got to play professional softball for a number of years before becoming one of the first player–general managers in professional sports. In my consulting career, I went from one exciting project to another, associating with some of the best and the brightest in business, government, and the nonprofit worlds, interesting people who were making major differences in their worlds. I built an organization I'm proud of, made a fair bit of money, accumulated some nice toys, and bought a house that I love. What wasn't there to like about nose to the grindstone?

Of course, I've mentioned the downsides I experienced in terms of poor health, lots of stress, lack of time, and some difficulties in my relationships. But our prevailing contexts are effective at keeping us on track because they give us plenty of positive feedback.

Jeanie Bunker's former context "not smart-pretty-good enough" is a much more malignant-sounding one, but it sure got her a long way. When a dyslexic girl from a dysfunctional family (as if there's any other kind) makes it all the way to the top ranks of one of the premiere information technology companies in the world, you know something has gone right. For Sally Crawford, "work hard, be nice" had its wonderful payoffs, too. She built a multimillion-dollar company that connected a host of employees and clients who all knew they could rely on Sally for absolutely anything. In the meantime, Sally got plenty of accolades, some amazing relationships, and all the prizes that go with success in business.

In fact, there's no reason—or certainly no motivation—to reveal and own our prevailing context until the downside begins to overwhelm the upside. As a human being, you milk that context for all its worth, or ride that sports car as far and as fast as it will take you. It's only when you run out of milk or hit the wall that you have any reason to look around and try to figure out why it's not working anymore and what needs to change to make things better again.

The Good News and Bad News About Your Context

Once you've done the work of revealing your context, I recommend that you seize the opportunity to take stock of that context by doing an audit of the upside and the downside. Think deeply about the intended and unintended outcomes. Use Table 2.1, put it all down on paper, acknowledge it, revel in it, laugh and cry. Then tack it up to your wall and be prepared to do something about it.

In Bug Soup

People have their sense of reality rocked when they realize that much of what they see and understand about the world is based on their lifelong, factory-installed contexts. The shock can leave

Table 2.1 Your Context Audit

Upside *Deliberate Choices and Positive Results*	*Downside* *Negative Outcomes*
Work	Work
Dreams	Dreams
Relationships	Relationships
Health	Health
Finances	Finances
Belongings	Belongings
Worldview	Worldview
Other	Other

Upside *Unforeseen Benefits*	*Downside* *Unintended Consequences*
Work	Work
Dreams	Dreams
Relationships	Relationships
Health	Health
Finances	Finances
Belongings	Belongings
Worldview	Worldview
Other	Other

them humbled, lost, and momentarily powerless, a feeling that leaders in particular are completely unaccustomed to after a life-time of assertiveness.

For that reason, many leaders have a tendency to skip over the "own" stage of revealing and shifting context. They like to glance at the ledger, close the books, and say, "Okay, I get it. Now let's move on." But you need to get deep inside your old context first. You need to contemplate the upside and the enormous value you mined from it. You need to dwell in the downside, examine those unintended consequences, and contemplate the casualties that have arisen as a result. Doing that deep work is the only way to reach the critical threshold where you finally realize that the compelling need to design a new context trumps the compelling pull of your historical context. Your default context is so strong and so embodied that it's always there to claim you. I liken it to a game of Red Rover. You're standing in the line, facing your past, and it calls you back over. You heed the call, run like hell, and get trapped in the arms of those you know only too well.

Dwelling on your old context can feel like a waste of time. It's not. It's a period of retreat during which you are releasing the physical structure of a lifetime of old habits, while new possibilities are forming. I compare the experience to what happens when a caterpillar wraps itself in a cocoon and prepares to become a butterfly. The depth of change the caterpillar undergoes is a little like being reborn. Inside the cocoon, the caterpillar doesn't simply grow wings and change its shape. Instead, it dissolves into liquid, a kind of bug soup without shape or form. After a while cells begin to regroup, then those new collections of cells form new shapes, like the butterfly's beautiful wings.

The regrouping and reforming that goes on in your brief period of mental retreat is essential to the transformation that follows. Once a new, self-determined context is set, people begin to emerge from the cocoon. The world seems blazingly fresh all of a sudden, but there's a sense of fragility and tenuousness that can leave one feeling awkward and incapable. It's no time to be forcing anyone to soar. When a butterfly emerges from its cocoon, its wings are crumpled into a wet tangle. Anyone who wants to help the butterfly by accelerating the process and pulling its wings straight would be doing tremendous damage. The wings would in fact be permanently malformed. The butterfly needs time to dry and stretch and let the sun and the air teach the wings how best to work. But once that has happened, the beauty is there for all to see.

Individuals and organizations experiencing profound change go through a similar sense of formlessness and helplessness for a time, followed by a period of uncertainty in which new skills and habits need to be allowed to set before they take flight. To change your world, your career, and your life, the place to start is within. Drilling down through the layers to understand the core of who you are and why you act the way you do reveals the essential material that is yours to shape the way you see fit.

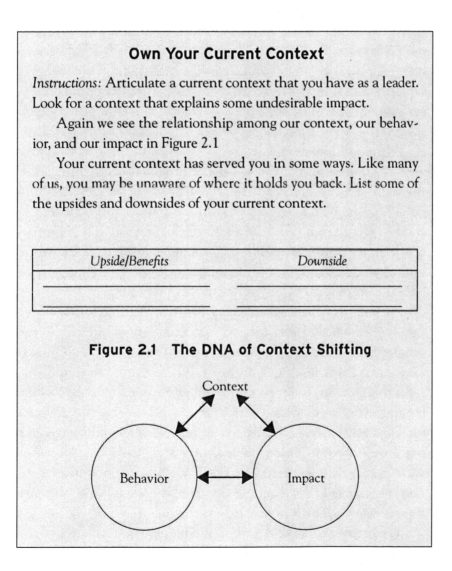

Own Your Current Context

Instructions: Articulate a current context that you have as a leader. Look for a context that explains some undesirable impact.

Again we see the relationship among our context, our behavior, and our impact in Figure 2.1

Your current context has served you in some ways. Like many of us, you may be unaware of where it holds you back. List some of the upsides and downsides of your current context.

Upside/Benefits	*Downside*

Figure 2.1   The DNA of Context Shifting

Context

Behavior   Impact

Not as Smart as Everyone Else So Have to Work Twice as Hard

At the age of forty, Grace Winters was made executive vice president of a $500 million division of a medical services company. She'd barely taken on profit and loss responsibility in her previous managerial position, but her leadership skills and creative talents catapulted her to exalted heights. Grace worked hard to live up to the expectations and responsibilities of her new role during the next few years. She excelled despite the fact that the industry was going through very tough times. Cash became tight in her company. Grace had to shift her focus from creative entrepreneurial endeavors to an operational obsession with the bottom line. The company slashed the advertising budget and reduced spending drastically.

Although Grace continued to excel in her role as executive vice president and got praise for her financial acumen, it wasn't the kind of work that made her feel excited or passionate. She'd gone from being a magician of marketing to a bean counter. She tried to resign, but her boss asked her to stay on. The company was looking to merge with a larger competitor, and they needed Grace's steady hand for a while longer. She agreed to hang on and help the employees through that transition period.

At the eleventh hour, however, the merger fell through. Employees who'd been told to expect the best out of the new arrangement were demoralized by the return to old problems, and Grace was stuck leading a division that remained in limbo. As a reflective person, eager to improve her ability to manage a challenging set of circumstances, Grace looked outside the company for some advice and coaching. She turned to me, and I agreed to come on board provided I work with her entire team as well as with Grace. From experience I knew that the division itself would need to engage in some serious context shifting in order to deal as a group with the turmoil it had gone through.

We began the work together. I explained the concept of context shifting and led the management team through the challenge of revealing their own personal contexts and the context of the group. Grace distilled her personal context down to a simple but acute statement: "I'm not the smartest person in the room so I have to be extra-prepared." There were a host of unintended consequences to that prevailing context. For instance, Grace quickly became annoyed at people around her who didn't prepare. There was one manager in particular who was so bright she felt that she could take on projects without any advance work and still pull everything off. Understanding her own context helped Grace understand the reasons she had so many emotional disagreements with that manager. On an individual front, Grace recognized that she was undervaluing her own intelligence and capability, even as she was putting in extra-long hours to stay on top of her job. For someone who had great confidence in her creative abilities, Grace was uncertain about her financial and operational skills, so she spent all of her free time on nights and weekends going over financial reports and preparing for meetings. The grind of doing that heavy lifting was wearing her out and sapping her spirit.

Once she'd discovered the existence of her prevailing context, it was easy for Grace to recognize where she'd learned to adopt it. In her case, this inheritance, though created early in childhood, really became amplified in college. She grew up in a working class neighborhood in Baltimore, Maryland. Her parents understood the value of education but weren't highly educated themselves. Dinner conversations were not filled with political debate or artistic discussions, and Grace recognizes now that she developed a very narrow view of the world. Nevertheless, she was a confident young girl with occasional moments of shyness. She was the president of her school choir, the one who stepped forward to speak to parents about schedules and issues. She was always the brightest in her class, and she hated to be wrong. Once her math teacher returned her test docked by only one mistake. Grace redid the question, determined that it was the math teacher who was wrong, and had the mistake corrected to give her the perfect score she'd been expecting.

Grace's confidence in herself and her place in the world got rattled, however, in her junior year of college, when she transferred to Cornell. Suddenly, she was no longer automatically the top person in her class in a sheltered and uncompetitive environment. Now she was thrown into a competitive game, surrounded by roommates and classmates who had grown up in very intellectual and wealthy families. Grace felt terribly unsophisticated in comparison. The shock was intense, and in response she started working very, very hard to compensate. While the people around her had fun, Grace studied. In her senior year, her thesis paper became all-consuming. She worked on it over many weekends and throughout spring break. She got an A. It was proof that for someone who was "not the smartest person in the room," being overprepared was the only solution.

In her senior thesis, she wrote about the impact of prenatal education on pregnant mothers in the developing world. Grace was an idealist who wanted to do good for women. She chose marketing for her career, because she believed it would help her gain the skills to spread information widely. Her first company supported her faith in the value of being overprepared. Late nights at the office were prized. The most successful people were highly competitive dynamos who went from project to project in a whirlwind of new challenges. Grace soared.

Years later, when she was executive vice president of the medical services division at a company going through tough financial times, Grace came to appreciate how much the creative energy of her early work suited her personality. She liked nothing more than leading a small team of creative people in a skunk works-type project, under the radar screen, on a grand mission, aiming to beat the odds. Squeezing costs, cutting back, and steadying a ship in rough waters were tasks that she could effectively perform, but they did nothing for her sense of spirit or accomplishment, and they did not inspire her feelings of leadership. She knew she needed a change.

Shifting from What Doesn't Work to What Does

When Grace finally resigned from the medical services company, she was fully versed in the language of context shifting and knew that she was entering a period of retreat and reflection prior to developing a new context she hoped would better suit her going forward. On her own, she developed some tools and processes to make that journey from one context to another easier to navigate.

The first thing she did was to select open-ended goals or principles to guide her in making decisions about her life. She used her time in the bug soup to reflect and hone three principles that would be important for her to stick by in order to change her old context and embrace a better one.

1. Slow the Pace and Enjoy the Moment. Like many business-people and most executives or leaders, Grace was capable of doing many things at once and running through life at top speed. That didn't mean this ability should be supported and rewarded. To be a happier person and a more effective leader, she knew that less was more. She needed to be able to observe, reflect upon, and understand what was happening around her in order to make better choices for herself and the people who depended on her.

2. Make Myself a Priority. Again, like many successful and driven people, Grace found it easy to sacrifice her own personal needs and desires for the sake of others and the job. This approach was depleting her personal resources, robbing her of enjoyment in life, and ultimately reducing her effectiveness as a leader.

3. Seek Respect Over Being Liked Even If It's Uncomfortable. Grace realized that as a leader she was often more concerned with being liked than with doing the right thing. That urge manifested itself in a lot of different ways. She was not comfortable confronting people over difficult issues. She was prone to be overly accommodating. She did not always hold people accountable.

She realized, however, that at the end of the day, being liked is a very temporary feeling, while being respected is longer lasting and deeper.

In the bug soup, Grace slowed down. She spent a lot of time with herself. She read books, both fiction and nonfiction. She absorbed her reading in a new way, picking up ideas and signs in an unusually receptive state of mind. She did not feel any sense of despair, even though she had no idea what was going to transpire for her in the future. She knew, somehow, that everything would work out. She wanted to give herself the freedom to be creative and invent something better in order to make a difference in the world doing something she was good at. She was confident her guiding principles would help her evaluate whatever opportunities came her way.

She did not want to fill up the new sense of empty space in her life with random noise or mindless activity. She knew that many people work too hard to dig deep when they want to make a change. Grace wanted to be deliberate, conscious, and thoughtful, unafraid to be alone and reflective rather than active and engaged. Her days became occupied by simple tasks. She rode her bike a lot. She did fun things with friends, like going shopping or to a spa. She went for long walks with her husband, talking. She wrote frequently, consistently, and extensively in her journal, recording the moods she was in, the ideas that occurred to her, impressions about life. Some friends were concerned about how little she was doing with her life, but she resisted any pressure. After having run a $500 million enterprise, her new accomplishments included holding a particularly challenging yoga pose, meeting a friend she hadn't seen in a long time for coffee, or writing five pages in her journal. She realized her conscious choice to change was taking hold when a friend from her "past" life met her for lunch and remarked on how relaxed and content she seemed. Slowing down and taking stock allowed her to see that comment for what it was—an important marker along the road of a longer journey. Each night, before she went to sleep, she mentally recalled everything that had happened to her during the day: What time did she wake up, what did she do? It was a nice way of starting to value everything that happened to her and a big change from the intensity of going to sleep each night worrying about the ten things she would have to do the next morning.

She didn't allow herself to skip over the outcomes and unintended consequences of her previous context. She did a careful audit of the costs and benefits, and came to recognize even more clearly that her context was creating judgments about others and herself. Some of those judgments were incredibly trivial. She was obsessed with perfection. Typos in a presentation killed her. *How could she miss that mistake?* She'd even stopped having dinner guests because she didn't have the time to make perfect plans or create some extraordinary dish. On the upside, she also began to appreciate the wonderful things her upbringing had provided. She may not have been raised in the most sophisticated environment in the world, but she could relate to people from all backgrounds. She was determined, savvy, creative, and firmly grounded. She came to understand that a person's fundamental characteristics can be a strength or a weakness depending on the situation they find themselves in. It was another reason why being present and aware was so important.

There were two other things that Grace did to help her through bug soup. The first was to schedule time with a thought leader at least once a month or create some significant learning opportunity. The other advice was to share her feelings rather than grow isolated. "Sharing our experiences is part of what gets us through difficult or stressful times," Grace notes. "Sharing helps you realize that you're not some freak of nature, that we all have insecurities, and we're driven by certain beliefs about ourselves." By sharing those concerns with people close to her, Grace was able to see much more clearly how much her context "permeated so many things I did, my behaviors and attitudes and how I perceived others. I think that was the biggest reveal for me, and then it was the work of, where do I want to go?"

Trade Up to Being a Magician

In her new context, Grace wanted to shift herself to a place where she could unleash her creative genius and help herself and others realize their full potential. In making her new context real, Grace had two criteria in mind. First, "I wanted to be who I am, rather than someone I felt like I needed to be. That was a real awakening. It's not fun when you're not being authentic. It's hard to be your best when you're not being yourself. That realization was one of my key takeaways from my journey." Second, she knew she wanted to be more creative and entrepreneurial again in the service of something she believed in. She'd been happiest in her career while working on small projects, with little money, a tight team, and an important cause. "So, I decided I was either going to do something entrepreneurial or something more philanthropic. I wanted to leverage my idealistic mind-set." In a way, she wanted to return to the reasons she got into business in the first place.

For a long time she did not know exactly what role she would find to allow herself to engage with work and life in such a way. But she knew that her guiding principles would help her evaluate the options. It was completely unexpected, however, when her dream job suddenly dropped in her lap, and she was hired to lead a global nongovernmental organization (NGO) committed to economic sustainability.

"To some degree, I think it was divine intervention that this job appeared in front of me. I can't think of any other reason why the position had been open so long, and they were looking for someone with my background in marketing, and I just happened to show up." Her friends and husband couldn't believe how timely and fortuitous it turned out to be.

Because of her careful work in building her new context, Grace was well-prepared mentally and spiritually when she assumed her new position. "Coming into this job, I felt so much wiser." She didn't know a lot about the NGO world—a concern that would have forced her to cram and learn in her old mind-set. Instead, she walked in the door from day one knowing she didn't have to be the smartest person in the room. "I introduced myself in all those meetings by saying, 'I'm a complete student. I have a beginner's mind. I'm coming in with some knowledge based on experience, and a framework for how I do things, but I don't have all the answers.'" Her stance helped foster some great conversations. Within two weeks, she was able to frame an "early thoughts" document and began shopping it around the philanthropy community. Receptions were positive when she discussed how she was thinking about the work of the organization and how she intended to approach the sustainability issue philosophically rather than loading up on specific details. People couldn't have been more welcoming. But she knew it was better to be respected than liked. Grace knew she hadn't come on board to be a nice person, but a social activist leveraging the agency's resources to drive change.

As a leader who had done some personal context shifting, Grace recognized that her new team was operating under a prevailing context that was limiting the scope of what they could accomplish. "They had a lot of talent, but they were living in a very old context in the NGO world that I call the 'check-writing' context." Relying on Jungian archetypes as metaphors for the change she wanted to create, Grace talked to her team about shifting from being "altruistic do-gooders" to becoming "magicians." She told them that the power of economic sustainability lived in the hearts and minds of all people rather than in the agency. They needed to tap into and channel that power by creating possibilities. As Grace pointed out, the agency was a team of twenty-seven people, but the potential donors were in the millions. "We need to marshal people's energy and engage their passion to start doing the right things for the planet." In order to make that happen, her team had to start thinking like a partner or consultant to the public and bring a more disciplined and strategic mind-set to their work.

The challenge of changing the do-gooder context and engaging the power of partnership was a thrill for Grace. Her difficult experiences in her previous job gave her great confidence and a sense of wisdom. She excelled at strategic visioning and inspiring an organization to get behind that vision. She was now more effective as a leader in terms of guiding people in operationalizing her vision. Moreover, she felt authentic and engaged. "I feel like I bring my whole self to work every day," Grace says. "I don't compromise a bit of who I am. I feel that my compassionate and collaborative leadership style is so powerful in this job, where it might have been a detriment in my past role."

Soon after Grace took her new position, a tsunami struck Asia, taking hundreds of thousands of lives and devastating communities. The world response to the disaster was tremendous and overwhelming. Everyone wanted to help. It would have been easy to just start frantically fund raising and help out in the traditional way. But the organization spent time listening to the concerns of experts in the field who advocated particular ways they could help in rebuilding the economies of local communities. Several years later, those efforts have had long-lasting impact. In retrospect, Grace believes she would not have been able to approach the crisis that way if she hadn't been able to slow down and listen, and the idea itself wouldn't have been seized upon if she hadn't created a tone and an organizational culture where a different kind of philanthropy could exist.

"That's what I feel philanthropy can do," Grace says. "It's about leveraging all kinds of assets as a vehicle to make a bigger social impact. And that's what I'm trying to bring to this organization. I'm trying to be the magician. I'm trying to set up the circumstances so the people can create their own brilliant ideas. I don't mind being the person behind the scenes making that happen. It's much more powerful when every person owns the success." For Grace, the opportunity to lead her team in changing the role of an NGO has fulfilled her greatest desire to make a difference. "I really feel like this job is taking everything I'm about and all the knowledge and experience I've gained and applying it in a way that I feel is doing something for good. It's so in tune with who I am."

The Journey of Trust

Grace Winters's story teaches us a lot about the dynamics that occur when an individual comes to recognize his or her personal context. It takes time, effort, and reflection to come to grips with that realization. Some people are fortunate to be able to have the opportunity to step off the track and make that shift in relative quiet. Others need to do their revealing, owning, and shifting on the fly. This is particularly the case with leaders of teams or organizations. As I've mentioned, leaders are in the context-shifting business. They work on their personal context consistently, as the need arises, becoming ever more aware of when tweaking, honing, or shifting is necessary. They also work on revealing and shifting context in others, individually and in group settings, all the time. If you can imagine, it can be immeasurably more complicated to encourage others to context shift in a work setting. In particular, our innate resistance to owning context is very strong. But there are a number of important techniques a leader uses to overcome the natural resistance to hearing the truth or being able to perceive issues in a radically different light. Ultimately, it's about creating an environment where trust is an abundant rather than a scarce resource. Those techniques include

- *Being centered and present* so that you are in the moment rather than distracted by other agenda items
- *Listening with curiosity* rather than a preset conclusion about the right answer
- *Accepting feedback* with a generous spirit, and
- *Assuming positive intent* as a way of granting trust before it is earned

No discussion about context shifting would be complete without examining the essential role of trust . . . trusting oneself, trusting others, trusting the process itself.

I'm probably not the first person you've heard discuss trust as existing on a continuum. On one extreme we have "earned" trust; on the other extreme we have "granted" trust (see Figure 2.2). Earned trust is such a ubiquitous expectation for us that it's hard to see that there might be any other kind. Simply put, *earned trust* means we come to trust in someone or something when expectations are met repeatedly over time. When another person does what they say they will do, reliably and repeatedly, they amass a "bank account" of trust with us. They have passed our test. They have proven that they are trustworthy. Even if they occasionally fail, it is seen as a hiccup or anomaly against a backdrop of reliable trustworthiness. This same criteria is unknowingly applied to ourselves. Look and see where you have passed the test with yourself. What areas are you reliable in, no matter what?

So, trust requires proof. Sounds like a reasonable truth, I bet, but it's only a conclusion. Earned trust isn't the only mode of trust you can operate from.

On the other side of the continuum is *granted trust*. Think of this as a gift of your trust. You haven't known the other person long enough to build up a bank account, so you "extend an unsecured line of credit." You assume positive intent and you expect the best possible outcome. Often times this kind of trust becomes more obvious in a crisis. Imagine that you go skiing with your child.

Figure 2.2   The Trust Continuum

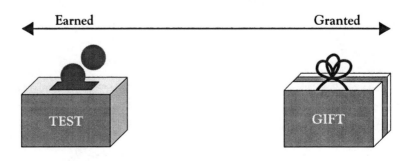

Table 2.2 Earned Trust Versus Granted Trust

Trust as a Test	Trust as a Gift
Deposit and withdraw (units in, units out)	Assume positive intent
Meet expectations over time	Expect the best possible outcome
Show me/prove it	Partner to ensure success

She collides with a tree and ends up sprawled out on the snow. Another skier quickly drops to her knees, declares she is a doctor, and begins to gingerly examine your most precious daughter. You don't know if the woman is in fact a doctor. You don't know if she graduated *summa cum laude* or at the bottom of her class. In that moment you grant her trust to do the right thing.

As is the case with earned trust, we have also experienced granted trust with ourselves. Remember trying something you'd never done before? In fact, although earned trust is our default form, we have all experienced earned and granted trust as well as everything on the continuum in between. (A comparison of the characteristics of earned trust and granted trust appears as Table 2.2.)

Operating in an environment of trust makes it easier to do context shifting. When I know that I am open to hearing other people's feedback without defending myself, when I seek others' points of view that don't necessarily match mine, then I know that I have entered a space of trust in which I will learn important things about what needs to be revealed.

Granted Trust

Let's look at an example of granted trust in the workplace. Gretchen McCoy is a leader who enabled her team to function at high levels of trust by getting them to own and create context shifts on an everyday basis. The techniques she used are as effective with individuals or in intimate relationships as they are in large groups. But the circumstances of Gretchen's success are amazing to learn about.

At Visa, the iconic payments system company, Gretchen was given the green light to overhaul the billing system that serviced 21,000 member financial institutions. Gretchen's vision wasn't just to rearchitect what was already in place but to bring in new technology, rethink how the organization was doing business, and make the future a whole lot better.

If there has ever been a project more tangled and knotted, I have yet to encounter it. I was called in to help facilitate the relationships toward achieving the project's goals. Known as a "dragon slayer" for her ability to tackle difficult tasks, Gretchen had the strategic skills and sales ability to see the need for the project, sell top executives on the concept, and get the funding. She likened it to starting a new business and getting venture capital funding to go forward. But turning vision into operational success was an enormously complicated undertaking. Each of the 21,000 member financial institutions was a customer with expectations that every transaction going forward would be handled correctly and properly, first time, every time. Servicing that customer base was "Visa corporate," with six regions around the world, each with their own chief financial officer, information technology department, and cultural contexts. On top of that, Visa relies on a completely independent but wholly owned subsidiary called Inovant to do its information technology work. Gretchen and her team were in charge—because she was ultimately accountable for bringing the project in on time and on budget—but she had to interface with a hundred other decision makers and executives to make that happen.

To get there, Gretchen and her team needed to be the bridge, the negotiator, the facilitator, the enforcer, and the translator. There were different regions and different cultures with different priorities. There were groups of people speaking the language of business and groups who spoke only the language of technology. In the meantime, Inovant, as the system developer, preferred to do its work outside the light.

The situation called for context shifting. "Something had to change," Gretchen says. "When you have a stressful situation, a project with a time limit and a cost element, and different regions, organizational structures, cultures, roles, and power plays going on, you need to wipe all that noise out and say, Hey, we're people working together toward a higher purpose." The relationship with Inovant was particularly critical. Gretchen knew she needed to create a sense of true partnership or the venture would never succeed. "I said, we're in this together. It's on our watch. Let's not make excuses, let's figure out what the problems are and find the solutions so we're all successful. We know the trust level is low, so how can we gain your trust?"

Gretchen's language is the language of context ownership. She was trying to establish a sense of ownership over the basic problems and difficulties that were necessarily going to be encountered, without creating an environment of finger pointing, suspicion, blame, and passive-aggressive defensiveness. It was necessary for her to do so because the dynamics of trust are not easy, particularly in stressful situations. Indeed, when it comes to trust, corporate America is a land of survival of the fittest. Absent any design or intervention, the only trust that gets established is trust that is earned. Typically, people have to prove they're trustworthy before they are trusted. Unfortunately, few project teams and few organizations have the luxury of waiting for trust to take root. It needs to grow like a wildfire.

I Not Only Heard You, I Listened

So how does trust get established at an accelerated rate? One critical tool is *listening with curiosity and fascination* rather than through the filter of a preset conclusion. Leaders are slowly learning about the importance of listening, but they still have a long way to go. The traditional view of leadership is that leaders are in the business of "telling people what to do." Being a "switch thrower" means being someone who can make decisions about whether to hire, fire, or promote another person. It doesn't matter whether you **would** fire or demote someone—the fact that you have that power shapes what people will or won't say around you. This gives a leader a lot of coercive power, but it doesn't make the job of leadership any easier.

We're stuck on the notion that a leader's job is to *know* and to use his or her superior knowledge to direct others. In this context, information comes to be a valuable and hoarded commodity. But if knowledge is the key to authority, then it's only natural for a leader to guard and protect knowledge from others and dole it out only in sufficient quantities to get the job done, but not so freely as to make anyone else knowledge-rich. Further, each person on a task or project should only be given what they need to know for their part of the project, and only one person, the leader, should have information that crosses functional lines and encompasses the project as a whole.

In their book *The Communication Catalyst*, authors Mickey Connolly and Richard Rianoshek show that collaboration is the root of innovation, creativity, and groundbreaking progress. Like other recent leadership theorists, they go on to suggest that effective leadership consists of listening and learning. In fact, effective leadership occurs when the leader creates a context in which listening, learning, idea sharing, and feedback can take place in an atmosphere of high trust.

"I heard every word you said! How else could I tell you what's wrong!"

There is a world of difference between hearing and listening. We hear because sound waves impact our eardrum, setting off a chain of events that culminate in activity in the auditory cortex of our brain. But hearing, or *sensation*, is only the first action in listening, or *perception*. The unexamined view of perception is that it is a mirror of sensation in much the same way that a camera makes an objective record of visual data. We assume that our perception captures the actual physical world, but those who have studied perception know that nothing could be further from the truth. Rather than a camera, our perception functions as the gateway for our personal context—a set of filters on what we hear. The filters are based on past learnings, past experiences, emotional reactions, and so on, and function outside our awareness or before conscious analysis has a chance to take place. Connolly and Rianoshek use the term "fast past matching" to describe this; others use the term "automatic listening."

Whatever we want to call it, our default listening context is essentially binary in nature. It sorts what we hear into categories of right or wrong, good or bad, familiar or unfamiliar, agreeable or disagreeable, and so forth, all of which are judgments based on the past and our personal context and severely limit any possibilities for creativity, innovation, and achievements that are inherently future focused.

There is, however, another way for leaders to listen, known as "generous listening." It is based on three filters: accuracy, interest, and learning.

Accuracy entails sorting out facts from conclusions, opinions, explanations, and interpretations. Facts are observable, verifiable events. They are real (as opposed to fantasy), evident (independent evidence can be gathered to prove their existence), and demonstrable (they can be shown to another person). Anything that fails any of these tests is not a fact, but a *conclusion*—an explanation, opinion, or interpretation. Accuracy is difficult to assess. In everyday conversation, we generally do a poor job of distinguishing facts from conclusions. When we look out at the evening sky and say, "That sunset is beautiful," we have a tendency to treat the information "beautiful" as being on a factual par with the information "sunset." But when we parse the phrase and point out the soft spots, it's immediately obvious that beauty is a conclusion and sunset is a fact. In practice, however, very few people treat or think about these two pieces of information as being different. That may sound like a trivial example, but you can quickly imagine other conversations in serious matters. "That manager is not being helpful," contains two different kinds of information, as does "The goal is impossible."

Interest is a critical factor in every successful conversation. To listen with a genuine curiosity and interest in what the other person is saying opens everything up and creates more possibility than a parachute drop full of money. When we listen with a preformed conclusion in mind, we create automatic assessments based on what is already known or familiar to defeat or mute the energy of another person. Instead of shutting down or mentally shouting down what a person is saying, a leader needs to question assessments that are automatic by asking him- or herself, "What does this person see that I don't? How are they looking at the world that helps them form that conclusion?" Such questions need to be asked, not with incredulity, but with openness and generosity to allow for the possibility that the other person sees something the leader does not, and that what they see may be valid and useful. If you could pretend, for a moment, that the person you are talking to is not a colleague or a direct report or a vendor, but a thought leader, an experienced contributor, a star performer—how much more interested would you be in what they had to say? I suggest that you would be capable of deriving more from that conversation than if you simply shut down the 80 percent of your brain that goes to sleep when you begin a conversation from the context that this person is going to say nothing that will impress me, help me, or change the way I do business. Openly considering "What's possible in that idea? Where could that line of thinking take us?" will help the leader assess the information in a creative or generative way rather than a reductive or negative way.

The output of assessing for accuracy and listening with interest is *learning*. Learning is a natural consequence of being willing to hear rather than presupposing what you know. Leaders are learners, and they help others learn, too. The way a leader listens has a powerful impact on performance, not just on the individual, but of the team, because the act of listening is such an effective tool for revealing, owning, and shifting context.

A comparison of the approaches of automatic listening and generous listening is provided in Table 2.3.

No matter what position you hold in an organization—executive, manager, consultant, or individual contributor—you spend most of your day in conversation. If we use a broad definition of "conversation" to include e-mails and memos, voicemails and meetings, then an argument could be made that conversation takes up close to 100 percent of the day. We spend a great deal of that time listening automatically, failing to distinguish facts from conclusions, and not learning anything we did not already believe to be true.

Other people are sensitive enough to pick up how we are listening to them, just as we are sensitive to their demeanor. The effect of this kind of feedback loop is a constant cycle of disagreement and defensiveness that eats away at the core of relationship and collaboration and ultimately suppresses performance and innovation. How much better is it to view each conversation as contributing to a building up of ideas, solutions, and trust? We don't live and think in isolation from each other—we're connected through waves of energy. Conversations are like the violinist's bow sending tremors of vibrations into the air. Whether those vibrations cre-

Table 2.3 Automatic Versus Generous Listening

Automatic (Binary) Listening	Generous Listening
Right/Wrong	What could make that possible?
Win/Lose	What could come from this?
Agree/Disagree	What could that allow us to do?
Fit/Doesn't Fit	How can that contribute?
Good/Bad	What commitments could that idea advance?
Either/Or	Say more about that....
Realistic/Unrealistic	What do you see that I don't see?

ate wonderful music or annoying screeches is entirely in your own power.

The Feedback Sessions

Gretchen McCoy understood the importance of listening with accuracy, curiosity, and learning when it came to her immense and complicated project. She recognized that trust was low, and that, as she put it, "when you're under stress and everything's ready to blow up in your face, you tend to be knee-jerk and jump to conclusions." On a frequent and consistent basis, she convened feedback sessions with key members of the project team in attendance in order to prevent breakdowns and keep the project rolling.

Feedback, in corporate America, does not have a good reputation. Providing feedback is supposed to be a manager's or leader's job, through the vehicle of coaching or the annual performance review. But how often do we provide feedback well enough that the person receiving it feels genuinely grateful for the information? Not very. At best, we swallow our pride and thank the feedback provider because we know we are supposed to do so. But deep inside, we feel trampled on, misunderstood, and interpreted in the stingiest terms. In other words, absent any better methods, we suck at feedback, both the giving and the receiving of it.

Gretchen's feedback sessions functioned in an entirely different way. She created an alternate universe where, instead of disagreement and defensiveness, every idea, question, or piece of information built constructively on the last. The ground rules were based on the kind of listening necessary for context shifting. She started each meeting by saying, "Let's put all the things that aren't working right now, up on the board, for everyone to see." She then established an open environment to hear the good, the bad, and the ugly, by permitting everyone to call out any instances of finger pointing, blame, and excuse making, while praising demonstrations of responsibility, mutual understanding, and innovative solutions. Every statement by every individual was met with genuine interest; facts were clearly distinguished from conclusions; and conclusions were held lightly and ready to be surrendered at the first hint of a new or better view. It was necessary to create this kind of dialogue because new information was critical in an ever-evolving project plan, and frustrations, pent-up emotions, and stale ideas would have been overwhelming without the fresh breeze of generative conversations. "Just like in any relationship in life," she notes, "you need to listen really intently to the other person's perspective and learn where they're coming from because everyone has good ideas, and they're seeing something you're not, and you want to understand that. As partners, you need to put your heads together and come up with a solution, rather than being emotionally tied to anything."

Gretchen led the way in these feedback sessions by putting herself forward as a model receiver of feedback. She had been open about her plans and principles in leading the project team from the beginning, and she stated at each feedback session that she would appreciate whatever feedback people could provide to help her in the areas where she was not living up to those established principles. From the point of view of her subordinates and colleagues, Gretchen was in a powerful and potentially threatening position as the switch thrower of the project. Gretchen was aware of this potential pressure. "It was very courageous of people to say, 'Hey, you're wrong,' or to ask me if I had thought about things from another angle, or, to suggest that I was jumping to conclusions. It wasn't easy for them to call me on my stuff. But my reaction each time was paramount in how they would react again." Gretchen was super-conscious that she was teaching her team and reinforcing the old or the new context via her receptivity to feedback. She knew that it was critical to embrace the new way in order to sustain that context shift and build a trusting environment.

The process of receiving feedback is outlined in Table 2.4.

Table 2.4 Receiving Feedback

Make a request	Request feedback in a specific area of concern
Explore what matters	Explain what you care about and what you want
Receive the feedback	Listen through "this is not the truth" and ask clarifying questions
Ask for substantiation of the feedback	Ask what it is about you, your way of being, communication, or actions that produced that feedback
Ask about new action	Request suggestions on what new actions you can take or behaviors you can practice
Say thank you	Thank them for the conversation and their partnership

Assume the Best of Intentions from Others

Another critical piece of the puzzle in developing a trusting partnership was to encourage everyone involved to *assume positive intent*. What does this mean? Very simply, the one way to be receptive to another person's contributions, feedback, and speaking is to assume that he or she comes into work each day at least as committed as you are to make a difference. Believe me, this *is* the case.

The most common evidence leaders use for a person's lack of commitment is that he complains, drags his feet, or passively resists doing something. How often do we assume that he is not worth the time or effort of a true partner? But consider the possibility that people's complaints are their highest expression of commitment. If they didn't care or didn't think that things should be better, they wouldn't bother showing their dissatisfaction. Sometimes complainers are like the canary in the coal mine—they are the loudspeaker of the system revealing that something needs to be rethought, reengaged with, or redesigned. Listening to rather than dismissing complaints from the context of assuming positive intent creates a fundamental shift in the information that can be gleaned. Every human being is motivated by the commitment to make a contribution. What's more, if you give another person the same credit or benefit of the doubt that you would prefer receiving yourself, then it preempts your stingy tendency to make accusations or shift blame. In other words, you need to listen for the contribution when someone speaks rather than focus on the delivery or the context you yourself are operating in.

Owning Complaints

One of the project leaders who attended my course worked for a large telecom equipment maker that had a poor reputation with its customers. Projects weren't delivered to customers on time or to their specifications. Morale at the equipment company was low as a result. People constantly complained about the company's processes.

The project leader decided to take ownership of those complaints and improve the way her company worked with customers. She started by articulating to customers that the company was committed to improving project delivery time. Then her team formed a task force that included major customers. This context shift was critical—her most important relationship, that is, her customers, were included in the solution so that both the company and the customer became committed to improving the product delivered and preserving the vendor-client relationship.

The project manager also had to manage her relationships within the company, keeping everyone focused on the ultimate goals, not the pain involved in getting there. Some projects improved, and delivery times were cut in half. Other projects remained difficult. The key lesson was her recognition that complaints and low morale were messages of commitment. Once she assumed that everyone on her team came to work wanting to do good, her feeling of trust expanded, and her team in turn was encouraged. She used that same mode to listen to her customers, and it freed her to acknowledge that their needs were not being met. Because she built an improved relationship with those customers, the company retained them while it worked to improve its processes.

As I mentioned previously, trust in corporate America operates out of the context that it must be earned. Gretchen's work with her multifunctional team created an environment in which trust was granted from the outset. This in turn created a mood or environment in which it was safer to have authentic conversations as opposed to what passes for normal in the cesspool of office politics—conversations that cover your ass or somehow subvert the good intentions of others to provide yourself with credit or your colleague with fault or blame.

Agreement Versus Alignment

Visa is essentially a network of 21,000 member financial institutions coordinated by a central influencing body. It provides an extreme example, therefore, of a common trend: most organizations are no longer heavily oriented toward command and control; instead they are biased toward creating agreement as the optimal basis for moving forward. Organizations that are oriented in this way use *agreement*, or consensus, as their preferred means of making a decision. While consensus can work reasonably well in small groups, it can have serious flaws when applied in large organizations or in complex situations.

First, it is a very slow process, since every person in the group must have the opportunity to air his or her views and be convinced to enlist in the leader's view. In a strict consensus-building process, a single person can put the brakes on by withholding his or her agreement. Of course, out of group pressure or fear of reprisal, people usually give their assent to a decision while secretly continuing to disagree. These secret vetoes often slow down or derail the leader's agenda.

Second, as illustrated by Figure 2.3, there's the risk that the entire process might devolve to the lowest common denominator on which people can agree, thereby diluting the power of whatever decision needs to be made. If each letter in Figure 2.3 represents a different person, with their own righteous point of view, only those areas of overlap that represent what the group agrees on can be explored. And, if a group of people focus only on areas where they have common ground, then new ideas are not likely to emerge. The conversation will devolve to who is right and who is wrong rather than what else is possible that may not have been thought of yet. When organizations operate based on agreement, each addition brings less common ground; thus by design, agreement (concensus) kills possibility.

Achieving *alignment* is very different from achieving agreement. In order to achieve alignment, the facts that are relevant to the matter at hand must be determined; sorted out from opinions, conclusions, and interpretations; and then agreed upon. This becomes the base or foundation of facts on which the group then builds as it goes forward (see Figure 2.4). During that sorting-out

Figure 2.3   Agreement

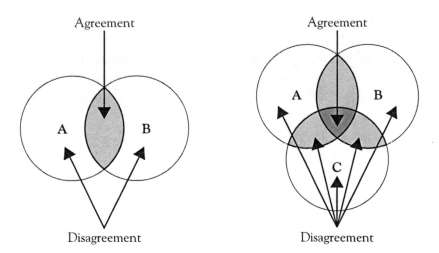

Source: Courtesy of Generative Leadership Group (www.GLG.net)

Figure 2.4   Alignment

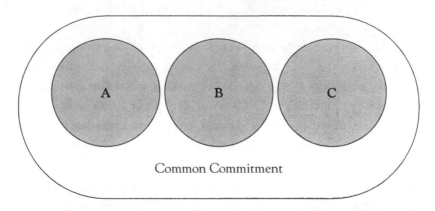

Common Commitment

time, everyone involved has the opportunity to state her personal agenda and to put any relevant concerns or worries on the table. The purpose of this initial discussion (which can be lengthy) is to discover where and how each person's purposes and concerns come together to form a common context. With alignment, there is no attempt to find common ground. Rather, the central issue is finding a common commitment in which to stand.

It is amazing what happens when people see that they share a common commitment. For instance, when I played professional softball I sometimes had to play next to people I didn't like. Because we had a shared commitment to win the World Series, we could find ways to coordinate action even if it wasn't my preferred way of turning the double play. The real question is, What do you all care about so much that you will gladly do what is required to move the group closer to that end even if it's not the way you personally would do it?

The dynamics that go on in the sorting-out process are interesting. From the beginning, each person feels free to voice an opinion, and this lowers resistance and reduces secret vetoes. Next, people feel they have been heard, which is the common and constant test for our sense of inclusion and trust. In the spirit of being heard, contributions are more deeply considered and valued. This improves the feeling of security and lets us know that we are safe to agree or disagree rather than be worried about more base concerns such as one's job being in jeopardy. Naturally, the sense of connection and belonging that results depends on the relationships of those involved. It also promotes an environment of learning and enthusiasm that the insights of the present can lead to better possibilities in the future. Finally, as a morale boost, it increases the sense each person has for be appreciated and improves feelings of loyalty, commitment, and trust.

When a common view has been achieved, the space for partnership, trust, and possibility has been enlarged. It's natural for everyone involved to experience a greater sense of ownership in the establishment of the project as a result. The clearest evidence that a common context has been established is that the conversation in the room migrates from one of sharing purposes and concerns to one in which ideas, new possibilities, innovation, and creativity flow freely. In the third phase of alignment building, these idea conversations naturally give way to a sorting process in which high-potential ideas begin to match up with realities, resources, and priorities for investing time, money, and human energy. The interim test for alignment is this process of investment. The ultimate test for alignment is successful execution.

Expanding the Circle

Gretchen's team finished their massive project on time and on budget. In my opinion, that accomplishment was truly a modern miracle. But those objective measurements were not used to assess the success or failure of their endeavor. Instead, from the outset, the success criteria were different. The team decided that they would know they had accomplished their objectives if, when they finished the project, they were all still talking to each other; and if, in the future, they would still want to work together on other projects.

Both those objectives were met. In fact, Gretchen's team was heralded not only for its incredible job at redesigning the organization's global billing system but also for the kind of culture it had created in the process. As Gretchen says, "They recognized the value of that, and they're expanding it to other projects." What's more, strong friendships and partnerships were formed among the team members, and there's a desire, now that the fruits of such partnership have been tasted, to have that kind of experience more often, if not all the time. This would not have been possible if the team hadn't taken ownership for their disempowering contexts about each other. The real courage they displayed in this project was to keep looking within themselves to see when and how they held conclusions that the other team members weren't as smart as they were, as committed as they were, or any number of similar contexts. Until they could see that they were the ones operating from "them versus us," there could have been no real progress. Owning our conclusions and perceptions about others is key to moving beyond their limitations.

The tools for listening, exchanging feedback, and the assuming of positive intent provided Gretchen's people with a mental model or a common language for achieving high performance. This capability is especially critical in today's flexible and change-intense organizations. Projects require leaders to work across boundaries and disciplines. Research and development needs to talk with marketing. People in the field need to talk to people at corporate. Context shifting provides a platform or operating mode from which to engage in common dialogue. It is also a means that one leader creates change in those around them. Otherwise, as many executive coaches have discovered, you can work on changing one person, only to see him revert or fail when he gets put back into the system. The culture exerts an enormous pressure on individuals. Without like-minded partners, you don't stand a chance.

Gretchen is not focused on personal wins or singing her own praises. But she gets a tremendous satisfaction out of coaching others and seeing them grow. "To me that's the ultimate," she says. "I don't need the trophy." Her team is exceptionally loyal to her because of the environment she has tried to build. "We just love working together. We've created a sanctuary or island, a very nurturing place, and we say that if you get beat up out there, you can always come back here and get rejuvenated." Recently, however, her new boss began to insist that she help spread her people and the partnership skills they've developed around the organization by encouraging them to work in other areas. She thought about it and realized her boss was absolutely right. "Letting them go was another learning experience for me. It's not that I discouraged it before, we just never talked about it. I asked them in performance reviews whether they wanted to look for something else, but they were always okay with staying. Then I started to look out for promotions or positions for them instead, and it was a different way to angle it." Now that some of her best people are working in other areas, she has come to appreciate the benefits of that migration. "It's neat, because we're still really close, but we're getting the magic out to other places."

Gretchen views it as a way of sustaining the context-shifting abilities she has helped foster. As a leadership strategy, it is also a way of scaling out and spreading the message, or the magic, into larger realms. As Gretchen puts it, "At the end of the day, the only way you're going to do business anywhere is to understand that you're all connected, and you're all working toward something. If you can't work together, it's not going to happen."

Listening Your Way Through

Of course, taking ownership for a context that was inherited or forged due to external circumstances is a tall order. How can you own an organizational culture or context that you didn't create? At the heart of ownership is the assumption that if it's happening on your shift then you have something to do with it. As my friend Ellen Wingard reminds me, "We are the arsonist in our own fire!" If I don't take ownership for my contexts, then I am destined to be a victim of other people and external circumstances.

Revealing your context can make you feel less certain because it shows you that the fundamental realities of life are constructs you have implicitly (probably unconsciously) agreed to and operate under. Your uncertainty is not a bad thing, but a good one. You have been temporarily freed from the tyranny of the unconscious. Like I said at the beginning, freedom is sometimes a scary or disturbing place.

While you are still in the unformed state between contexts—in the bug soup—it is critical that you use the tools of listening and feedback to own your context in all its warts and glory, while simultaneously generating the kinds of creative ideas necessary for you to generate a new context that will suit you better. Feedback provides all the big connections. It reinforces the clarity of your new thinking by showing you the benefits and unintended consequences of your prevailing context. In order to encourage and receive feedback, you need to slow down, be present, and listen. You need to sort facts from conclusions, put aside your preset agenda or beliefs, and put forward your curiosity. Learn. Assume that the person giving you feedback wants to make a spectacular contribution in your life. Grant trust around you freely, like a plant gives off oxygen, and you will be amazed at who comes forward and what gifts they have to offer you. In your world, you will create higher-level conversations that generate ideas and possibilities that were blocked off to you previously. And you will be fostering relationships and connections that will support your journey and help you in achieving your new context and using that context to make a difference.

No person, no leader, makes a difference alone. Not in herself, not in others, not in the world.

Up to this point in your life or circumstances, you've been running on autopilot. Now, you've got your hands on the controls. The willingness to own your prevailing context has given you the freedom to choose a more powerful context. So where do you want to go? The gift of uncertainty is that you become more open to other possibilities, other views, other versions. From this openness, you can learn to shape your own life with a sense of deliberation and purpose. In the next chapter we discuss Step 3, how you can be the author of your own life.

3

I AM THE AUTHOR OF MY OWN STORY

Step 3. Design a New Context

Trade Up to the Life You Want
Creating a new context moves me from being a product of my past to being the inventor of my future.

Why DESIGN?

- Infinite possibility in the face of any circumstance
- Others' engagement in my compelling future
- Dramatic increases in leadership and organizational effectiveness

> When nothing is sure, everything is possible.
> — *Margaret Drabble*

> Necessity is the mother of taking chances.
> — *Mark Twain*

When you come to the realization that the context you've long operated from is a conclusion about life that you didn't choose, a natural question arises: If I were in charge of my own life, what context would I invent to create the future I want? We call this choice point the "trade-up."

Step 3, the stage of context shifting known as "design," is both freeing and paralyzing. Often I ask people, "If you were really the author of your own life story, what story would you write?" Of course, the question is a trick. You *are* the author of your life story: the page is before you, the screen is blank. It's time to start writing. Intimidated? You bet. Very few of us ever have to confront the power of authorship. But if you ask any writer, you'll likely learn that the blank page can be a terrible and frightening tyrant, no matter what subject matter the writer aims to tackle. It is up to you to author your life for the next ten, twenty, or fifty years. Such an act is not for the faint of heart.

Where does your new context come from? Standing in the opening of having abandoned an old context, you find yourself wanting to create something else. In touch with your authentic self, you are at least temporarily able to embrace life in all its rawness. Suddenly, you gain a powerful sense of opportunity and responsibility—an utter opening compared to the narrow routine I refer to as "a near-life experience." Finally, and resolutely, it is your life to live.

At such times, I have seen profound changes in many people. The fastest, most massive behavior change I've ever witnessed took place in two seconds. I was watching a man named Kyle interact with his two children. Kyle was generally known as a complainer, a curmudgeon, someone who wasn't into displays of affection. But when I saw Kyle he was laughing, playing with his kids, and having a great time. Why the sudden difference? One two-second conversation changed Kyle's life forever: his doctor told him, "You have terminal cancer."

In a sense, that's the message I want to convey to you. We're all headed for the big nap. In fact, the nap could begin at any time. That's not a pleasant thought, so we avoid thinking about it, but if you were forced to reconcile with that inevitably, what choices would it offer? One conclusion you could derive would be that how you spend your life doesn't really matter—we all end up 6 feet under. On the other hand, awareness of your own mortality gives you an incredible opportunity to decide how to spend the time you do have. Think about the many compromises you make in your life, with your family, in your career, with your dreams. Think about all the times you settle for "close enough" instead of going for what you really want. Why? Life isn't a dress rehearsal, and there are ultimately no second acts. Once the curtain comes down, the show may go on, but you will not be part of the cast. Put in that context, the question becomes, What do you want to do with the rest of your life?

The Accidental Shift

Jennifer Higgins came to my program by accident, but the visit soon seemed preordained. In her mind, she was coming to the program because her favorite cousin had been participating in our curriculum for some time and wanted Jennifer to experience it. As a very senior executive in the banking industry, Jennifer had been through more than her share of management training initiatives over the years and was skeptical about embracing some new approach. But Jennifer felt touched by the fact that her cousin had reached out to her personally, and she decided to sign up despite her misgivings.

In the early part of the program Jennifer shared thoughts about where she was in her life and her growing dissatisfaction with work. Just giving voice to her concerns allowed Jennifer to realize that she was struggling more than she'd been able to openly acknowledge (Step 1, revealing). There had been signs of something going on below the surface. A year before, Jennifer had changed jobs, agreeing to a new executive position at a different company. Not too long after joining the new bank, Jennifer underwent a routine

360 assessment—receiving feedback from her manager, several of her peers, and her direct reports. She had participated in 360 assessments a number of times in the past, but never before had she received comments like "shrinking violet" and "hesitant to speak up in groups." Amazed, she wondered how that was possible and what it meant.

That change came to the forefront of Jennifer's awareness the morning we worked with the horses. The horse failed to respond to Jennifer's direction. The message to Jennifer was suddenly very clear. "I just don't feel confident leading any more!" she realized. The revelation helped her put into words a number of key events that had shaken her life recently. A short two years before, Jennifer's father had died. Jennifer had always been extremely close to her father—a role model and strong force in her life. A year later, her neighbor Jason, who was a close friend, succumbed to ALS. Jennifer had wanted to take time off from work to be with her friend during the final weeks of his life, but the end came much more quickly than expected. His sudden death was a terrible loss and shock. "Deep inside," Jennifer recalls, "I was beginning to confront that work had become more important than anything else. I had been shuttling back and forth between work and home and my Dad's bedside despite the challenge of raising a toddler and never made time with Jason a priority. After he died I really had to face the question of how I could have let that happen."

The questions only deepened as Jennifer reflected on the work environment that she'd inserted herself into. Her new work situation was very collaborative and nonconfrontational, an amicable workplace with a flattened hierarchy. While that may sound ideal in some management books, the reality wasn't a good fit for Jennifer's personality. She was team oriented, but she was accustomed to acting as a strong type A leader, someone who liked to direct others in a straightforward way, without overly relying on the more subtle artistry of influence and persuasion. She was also used to being singled out and rewarded for being extremely smart and reliable, for landing big deals, and for pulling off big, profitable new ventures. The rules were different in this new, highly political egalitarian environment. Although the company was rife with smart, technically competent people, Jennifer believed that too much was decided in quiet back rooms. What's more, the flattened hierarchy made it difficult to get things done and climb the ladder. After working with the horses and contemplating her flip from outspoken leader to shrinking violet, Jennifer came to some clarity about what was going on in her head. In order to adopt to a very different organizational culture and her new life pressures, Jennifer had been subconsciously working to suppress her assertive tendencies. As Jennifer put it, "I was actively trying to avoid being a leader."

The impact of that understanding was immediate (Step 2, owning). "I returned to work after the program and was shocked by what I had revealed to myself," Jennifer says. "I realized that I had paid a high price over the past several years—my peak, career upward mobility years. Suddenly, at forty-nine years old, I awakened to wonder, what was the golden ring I had been chasing?" Her job had kept her from the people she most wanted to be with. She'd felt as though she'd compromised on motherhood, sacrificed her health, lost valuable friendships, and put aside her deeper interests. What's more, although she'd been a leader all of her life, she was now behaving in counterproductive ways, suppressing her leadership as though she were ambiguous about whether she wanted to be in the game any more.

"Owning my context allowed me to shift the way I felt about it," Jennifer observes. Leadership had long been an incredibly important part of her life, a mode that she was used to operating in. But why did it matter? "It was a real awakening that enabled me to reevaluate my life and open up my eyes and heart," she reflects.

As Jennifer talked with the other participants about her leadership journey, some ideas about what she wanted to do and why she wanted to do them became increasingly clear. Despite not knowing exactly how she wanted to write her own future story, she was very certain about her desire to be a leader and use her leadership for some end. Once again, we entered the horse ring and Jennifer took her turn. This time, when she directed the horse around the corral, the animal moved beautifully, with a sense of purpose. "I saw my passion," Jennifer says, "and I realized that I had chosen to be a leader of my own free will, nobody made me! This is who I am meant to be, and I love leading. I don't do it because someone is forcing me to." Knowing that gave her a foundation of certainty. Now it was up to her to discover the impulses that would make her leadership meaningful again. It didn't take long, once she returned to her life and work, for Jennifer to come to terms with the context that had been revealed to her.

When she'd first visited our program, Jennifer had entered with a context in which her life felt as though it were being subsumed by work—her conclusion very simply was "achieving success at work is how I prove my worthiness in life." She now recognized the importance of bringing her leadership and life into greater harmony. "I wanted to reclaim my life and be happy again," she says. She began, after the workshop, by focusing on herself first. Her health was not great; her blood pressure and heart rate were too high. So she got back in shape, and began to eat better, and live a more healthy lifestyle. "I've lost 25 pounds since that workshop, and I plan to keep it going," she notes proudly. What's more, she found that by focusing on herself, she was enjoying different aspects of life more than she had in years. Before college, she'd been a competitive swimmer. She purchased a membership to her local YWCA and started swimming in the morning before going to work. "I love to swim now more than ever," she says with enthusiasm. "Losing the weight made it easier to move around and do the simple things in life. I felt so much better and even bought a new wardrobe!"

In terms of her work, Jennifer also began to understand how she could express her leadership in different and more satisfying ways. For years, she had been working as an operations executive in the financial services industry with a very international focus. With her recent career move, she's found herself working in community banking, a focus that felt both domestic and narrow. And yet, when Jennifer viewed that change through the filter of her new context, she realized she had come full circle in terms of her interests. As a college student, she wanted to be the president of the family-owned bank across the street from the campus. She loved the warm, friendly atmosphere that she felt whenever she went inside the branch. What's more, her new assignment in community banking gave her the chance to open up new markets, including rural locations and diverse market segments.

Jennifer felt rededicated to her work and reconnected to her passion. She set out to learn everything she could about community banking, setting up franchises, and giving people new economic hope. She found a way to assert her skills in making a difference.

"I realized that if I could rediscover what makes me tick, and find great ways to contribute that to others, then I could leave the world better than I found it, which is all I ever wanted to do." Jennifer also found some time to donate her skills to the Women's Entrepreneur Incubator at the YWCA where she swims. For someone who felt subsumed and used up by work, Jennifer now feels energized and rededicated while also taking great care to enjoy life along the way. It's a remarkable turnaround.

Not Just a Pendulum Swing

When Jennifer began her journey, she set out to achieve control and happiness in her life. Like many other people, she came to realize that suffering is optional. At every moment in life, you face choice points when you can choose to stay in the context that is causing you frustration and pain or shift to one that is filled with possibility. While Jennifer's choice was freeing and limitless in possibility, it was firmly grounded in the flow of her life thus far. She gave herself time in the bug soup and drew on her past experiences to create a new context that fit her better than she could have imagined.

Jennifer's new context did not mean moving wildly into an alternate direction by abandoning her career, throwing herself into nonprofit work, or focusing solely on her personal well-being—what's known as "the pendulum swing." Instead, in designing her context deliberately, Jennifer drew on what had been important for her in the past and used that rich resource to fertilize the renewed growth of old interests. "It was about having the courage and willingness to see how I was getting in my own way and then take responsibility for changing it," she explains.

To use myself as an example, having been "nose-to-the-grindstone Rayona," I could not decide that I would henceforth and forevermore be "laid-back Sharpnack." Instead, my new context—"It all turns out with grace and ease"—was informed by my past. It touched on my long-cherished desire to have more grace and ease in my life while still fulfilling my desire for achievement, connection, and service.

I had this pendulum discussion with an executive who realized that his prevailing context was "I look out for myself because no one else does." It was a natural belief system for someone who'd come from a hard-scramble background to climb his way up into exalted business heights. Nevertheless, the belief that he was only able to rely on himself was impeding his organization's success, and that he and everyone around him would be better off if he could shift to a more interdependent worldview. We both knew his new context could not be a pendulum swing away from that, a radical change in which he brainwashed himself to believe "I can always count on everyone to look out for me." Instead, as a leader, he could accept the idea that he needed to continue to rely on his personal strength, while becoming more conscious of the fact that he needed the support and creativity of others to achieve his objectives. As a result, the context we came up with was "While I can always count on myself, my greatest moments come through others." This preserved his core strength, while prodding him forward into a space where working with others created greater accomplishments.

A pendulum swing is not a creation, it's a reaction. A pendulum swing is a "not that." In other words, if you were swinging the pendulum you might say, "I'm not going to be a _____, as I was in the past." But that's not creation. An author doesn't write a book by determining the book he or she will not write first. Instead, the true artist is informed by past experiences, and the past work of others, to surpass former limitations and create something entirely genuine, authentic, expansive, and new. The context you design is a moving and expansive declaration of commitment that propels you forward without flinging you wildly out of orbit and into emptiness.

Though the context you design may get written on a blank sheet of paper, that doesn't mean it comes out of nowhere or is built on a nonexistent foundation. Your new context is informed by the past—by your experiences, passions, interests, dreams—but unlike your default context it isn't *generated* by the past. Remember, too, that your new context can't be a pendulum swing that brings you into direct opposition with your previous context.

The Calculus of Confidence and Competence

One thing that stops people cold when designing a new context is a belief that declaring the future is like making an empty promise. If you don't currently have the skills or capability to create a desired future, what's the point? In my experience, a surprising number of people in leadership positions suffer from this paralysis. They are plagued by the disconnect between competency and confidence. Do you know the feeling?

The truth is, few of us feel confident, and we have a natural tendency to wait for our confidence to build before doing something significant. Nevertheless, confidence grows only through practice, the ability to learn from mistakes, and the pride that arises through small wins. Think of the calculus of confidence in logical terms: most people wait for confidence before proceeding, but confidence is a result—not a prerequisite—that happens after you take risks. A lack of confidence in your ability to create the future should never hold you back from taking the necessary actions. Baby steps become giant strides that turn into superhero flight before you know it.

Sometimes confidence comes down to understanding for the first time that you already have the skills you need to achieve the future you want. One woman I coached worked as an administrative assistant at a large computer manufacturer. When she convinced human resources to fund her $40,000 tuition in a leadership training class, she thought it was an amazing coup. But the most shocking realization still awaited her. Once she began the course, she came to understand that everything she had done as a "mere" admin fulfilled the description of the role of program manager for her company's flagship product. Once she realized that she already did the same work that people two job levels above her did, she retooled her résumé to reflect those skills and applied for a program manager job. Immediately, she was promoted. Soon after taking on her new role and proving her capability, she was moved into a management position with direct reports. It all started with a change in thinking from "I support other people and I'm good with details" to "I know how to get things done while moving value along the work process chain."

My good friend Fran Zone taught me, "Stop auditioning for the job you've already got!" Ever wonder why, after years of experience, education, success, and positive feedback, you continue to overprepare for important meetings or refrain from leading when in the presence of others you consider more qualified, senior, or better suited? Perhaps your worst fear isn't that you're inadequate, but that you will succeed. After all, who are *you* to lead the project, find the solution, or direct the division? It sounds ridiculous when you let those crazy thoughts slip out of your own head or see them written on the page. But it can make you wonder who forced you to believe you needed someone else's permission to step forward? Could you, instead, give yourself permission to excel, to stand out, to do more than you thought you could?

If you don't feel worthy enough to work on your own concerns, think about the people around you. How can you expect any of your direct reports to step up and assert leadership if you don't model that capability? Who's going to show the people with untapped potential that more is possible? There's no better way for a leader to unleash the passion, commitment, and energy of others than by showing them how to make a difference.

Shifting from Certainty to Possibility

Consider how different your life, your team, your organization, or your community can be, depending on the context you use to view the future. It all comes down to your willingness and ability to invent conclusions that *expand your range of possibility* rather than narrow it. Contextual leaders view the same facts as everyone else, yet they draw radically different but equally plausible conclusions to determine a better future for themselves or their team, organization, or community. If a leader's ability is limited, that puts a lid on creativity, energy, and commitment and limits the scope of dreams and achievements. If the leader's context-shifting ability expands the range of possibility, something new and groundbreaking can occur as a result.

From Care-aholic to Empowering Leader

When I think of someone who has evolved courageously into new and very different contexts time and time again, I think of Gayle Dee. Gayle and I knew each other when we both played professional softball in the 1980s. She thought I was cocky. Go figure. Later, our orbits aligned once again when I was working as a leadership trainer and Gayle was a rising star at Genentech, the legendary biotech firm. Gayle had done her academic work in microbiology. She didn't want to work in a hospital but preferred research and running clinical trials. By the time I encountered Gayle a third time, when she attended our workshop, she was in senior management, supervising other managers.

Although Gayle was educated as a scientist, during the course of her career she'd become increasingly interested in how the culture or life of an organization impacted individuals. Like a lot of caring people working in organizations, Gayle was frustrated. Despite the important research being done at Genentech, she believed that people who had the passion to make a tremendous difference were being held back by the organization. Desperate to make some kind of change, she identified our executive leadership program as a perfect resource and asked her boss if she could get it funded. Ten thousand dollars for a three-month program seemed like an inordinate amount of money, but Gayle's boss signed off and Gayle came to see us.

Voicing her emotional state in the company of others was validating. Gayle was feeling burned out. She wanted a different life. She wanted to know herself spiritually and develop a relationship with someone she could love. Very quickly, she was able to put language to her feelings about what she wanted to accomplish and who she wanted to be as a leader. Soon she articulated a new context for herself, "By taking care of me I can be a better leader for others." This one would stick for the next decade: she decided she wanted to help others identify and realize their potential. That unfulfilled desire had been at the source of her dismay with the system. Looking at it another way, Gayle realized she wasn't just a frustrated manager but a "care-aholic." That was a big difference that helped her go back to work with a new orientation and a better understanding of her own emotional drivers.

At first, context shifting was not easy for Gayle. It required conscious and intentional practice, and it was virtually impossible to do without having a good support system of allies and friends. Nevertheless, Gayle was amazed at the power of context shifting to help her achieve her personal vision, so she decided to develop it as an intuitive and natural skill.

There were many occasions for Gayle to practice. Indeed, while making progress in her work, Gayle was also mindful of the other areas in her life that were needed to change. Spiritually, things started to coalesce. She'd been raised in the Midwest under the influence of three different churches—Lutheran, Presbyterian, and nondenominational—but had left them all behind. Now, she felt herself longing to reestablish a spiritual connection. Near her neighborhood in Half Moon Bay, California, there was a little pioneer church with a beautiful chapel. It turned out to be a Methodist congregation. Gayle walked in one Sunday, sensed the progressive community of the place, and felt at home—an experience that would have a major impact on her life. This community could be a perfect place to both take care of her own needs and be an empowering leader for other members of the congregation. Around the same time, Gayle met her future husband. That momentous happening provided another example of the way the future was generated by designing a context deliberately and looking for ways to make it come true.

Meanwhile, as a newly enlightened manager, Gayle had come to understand that "holding people back" wasn't an intentional strategy of the organization, but a kind of unintended consequence. She decided to seek an expanded leadership position because she thought she could make a difference in the organizational environment. Her current role was too narrowly focused to create the kind of organizational change she wanted to make. We brainstormed with Gayle about discovering a new playing field that could help her bring her leadership passion and skills into greater harmony. This time, when she went back to the organization, she asked to leave her post as a senior manager and be assigned the position of head of learning and development for the whole corporation. It so happened that the position had been open for a year, and the executives at Genentech thought she would be a perfect fit. They asked her enthusiastically when she could start.

Gayle had no experience in human resources or learning and development, so how did she imagine that she could step into the top role? As I mentioned a few pages ago, it all comes down to the calculus of confidence and competence. Gayle had oodles of competence. She had the right academic background and experience in the field as a research scientist. And she'd risen through the organization to become a manager of managers, empowering people to empower others. In other words, she knew plenty about learning and development, and she had tremendous insight into how that knowledge could be applied at Genentech organization-wide. This reinforced her courage and helped her step forward to assume a very different role.

Essentially, Gayle brought the technology of context shifting into the human resources function. In order to transform the cultural environment and make human resources a value-adding partner, Gayle assessed the context of her new department. Morale was low. Like the cobbler's children who wore no shoes, the people of HR were not used to being treated with the same nurturing respect they advocated in the field. Gayle changed that context, helping people to see the value they were creating through their services.

At the same time, Gayle set about creating a context shift within the larger organization. Genentech held several conclusions about itself that didn't withstand scrutiny. The first myth was that the organization was loaded with superstars. As Gayle puts it, some coaches in sports want to develop raw talent, while others want to manage top talent. Genentech believed its employees were all superstars, a view that obscured the need for managers to coach and empower. The second myth was that because only good scientists got promoted into management, Genentech was loaded with good managers. In fact, the skills that made someone a good scientist were entirely different from those that might have made her a good manager. Genentech's managers needed to be trained.

In shifting those assumptions, Gayle used communication and partnership as her tools. Along with her HR staff, she established a mode of conversation that was heavy on listening, enabling her team to pick up on the concerns of others in order to develop understanding and facilitate trust. "What can we do together to understand who you are?" became the mantra, but it also became a foundation for providing ongoing support. In a variety of situations, Gayle might come up with an idea for improving an aspect of the work environment, but she knew she needed partnership from the line in order to build that idea into a program with impact. She used the language of science and data to convince managers of the worthiness of a new approach and the importance of devoting some of their budget not just to product development but also to people development. She had the satisfaction of seeing a number of managers grow into leaders who were better equipped to develop talent in others.

Being the head of learning and development was an operational role, but Gayle loved the work of context shifting. As she explains it, "You get to capture the passions people have for their work, and you get to understand their language, to see it and personalize it." Nevertheless, she still longed to be more active on a personal level in identifying and helping other people reach their fulfill potential. Another context-shifting exercise helped Gayle reimagine herself as a coach. She had the experience and the demeanor but she knew she needed the training, so she went back to her superiors at Genentech and told them what she wanted to do. Again, they supported her, and Gayle got funding to be trained as an internal coach.

Soon, however, Gayle realized that working within a corporation was no longer where she wanted to be. As someone who'd seen a lot of change in others, she recognized her own midlife awakening and knew it was time to do something different. She set off on her own to seek out new experiences as a business and life coach. Her dream was to bring her context shifting and coaching to people from all walks of life by making her workshops affordable. She established a program and saw it succeed. Even so, the work wasn't as fulfilling as she'd hoped. Probing to understand why, Gayle recognized that she needed to do more to bring her growing spirituality into the mix.

Some years before, a young lawyer who'd abandoned her career for seminary training asked Gayle whether she'd ever thought about becoming a minister. At the time, Gayle had wondered what ever could have inspired the woman to make such a strange suggestion. Now, she saw the many ways that her work in business organizations helping others identify and fulfill their potential had parallels with work she could do in the church. Exploring these possibilities, she became even more involved in her little church. Soon, she was asked to start preaching to the congregation, but she didn't know how to begin. She'd always been a listener, not a speaker. Facing the issue of confidence over competence once again, Gayle understood that all she needed was "courage and a mouth." Her long-honed ability to listen helped her pick up on the concerns of the congregation and engage in a preaching dialogue that really touched on people's needs.

Gayle's work in her church has finally brought all her interests and passions into one circle. "One of the fascinating things you learn from contextual leadership," she says in retrospect, "is that it allows for enormous spectrum of viewpoints, and you can bring out who you really are." She has found that freedom in her progressive church community, and she sees her role as providing such support for others. "It is my job to create the compelling purpose for people to be here [in the church]. I can't mandate their choice, all I can do is create the environment where we engage in conversations [about faith and divine will] all the time."

This year, Gayle is graduating from the seminary and will soon be appointed somewhere in the country to serve as a pastor to her own congregation. She's traveled a long distance from her Midwest upbringing, her background in microbiology, her operational and leadership roles at the world's first biotechnology company, and her solo venture as a coach. I marvel at the way each successive opening was created by her curiosity. I admire the way her courage has led her to discover such wonderful new spaces, time and again.

Redesigning Yourself from the Inside Out

Designing your context is about putting a stake in the ground and declaring the future. The future doesn't even need to be in reach yet; but by declaring it, making a strategic plan to achieve it, developing the skills, tools and resources necessary, and enlisting support, you are stepping into that future in a committed way that will have tremendous impact on your ability to get there.

When President Kennedy made his famous challenge to "land a man on the moon and bring him back safely within the decade," that future was out of reach. We did not have a metal robust enough to withstand the heat of reentry without killing the astronauts. We did not have a fuel light enough to allow us to launch a spacecraft, land it on the moon, and land it safely back on Earth. Nevertheless, once the goal was set, the strategy, resources, and tools to achieve it were developed. Getting to the moon was a miracle—but it was a deliberately constructed miracle, one of millions that have happened in our lifetime.

You need to walk before you can run. Slow down. You are not going to create your new life in an instance of inspiration. It takes time and methodical strategy to get there.

For the Sake of What?

You'll remember from Step 1 that the most important question to ask is, "For the sake of what" would you devote your time, energy, and effort to reveal your prevailing context, take full ownership of its virtues and impediments, and design a new prevailing context? Let's be honest here. Most of us could milk our current (albeit default) context for the rest of our lives and do perfectly well. Given how powerful an engine my nose-to-the-grindstone context was, it certainly had a great deal of shelf life before it (and I) expired.

"For the sake of what" is the vision, purpose, reason, or cause that makes doing the hard work of context shifting worthwhile. It's the price we would pay in lost relationships or lost opportunities if we chose not to trade up and reinvent ourselves. In order to bring into focus that vision and the costs of not pursuing it, ask yourself a few questions:

1. If you had unlimited time and money, what would you do?
2. What legacy would you like to leave for your family, your team, your organization, your industry, your community, and the world?

3. What would you consider to be a life well lived?

4. What would you want as your epitaph?

5. What seems impossible, but if you could make it happen, would light up your life?

6. What is it that you want to happen "on your shift"?

7. What change effort would you be thrilled to lead?

8. What would you do if you knew you could not fail?

Thinking about such questions can seem like heady stuff. But you've accomplished great things in the past, even though you may forget how impossible they seemed at the time. When did someone tell you that something couldn't be done, and you did it anyway? What amazing accomplishment did you pull off out of sheer will and intention? Once we have determined what to us is a game worth playing, it is easy to see how trading up can contribute to and accelerate achieving that vision.

Becoming the Author of a New Story

As you design or articulate your new context, let your imagination run free to think about the opportunities that are available to you. You can choose to play a game called "being a loving and thoughtful parent" or the one called "leading my team to great achievements" or the one called "ending poverty." You can work on curing cancer, comforting people who are less fortunate, ministering to spiritual needs, or raising funds for a new community center. The choices go on forever.

On what basis should you choose? Is there a "right game" for you? To discover that game, it is necessary, as I've said, to go through Steps 1 and 2: the arduous task of revealing your prevailing context and owning it fully. Only then, when you have created that vacuum, will you have the clarity to see the new context you want to design. It takes days, sometimes weeks or even months. Be willing to float in the bug soup. Keep your friends and allies close to help you. Allow your thoughts to take time to coalesce. Scribble down your meandering ideas as you journal, and experiment with phrases that can contain the poetry of a newly articulated context. Resist the urge to replace your old context with something that may be ambitious or idealistic but is not connected to your authentic self or your real passions.

You'll begin to feel your new context in your body and your heart, and you'll know you have it when the words come to you. Language, after all, is the code by which we create reality. At first your new context may materialize as just a partial phrase. For me, it was the words *grace and ease* that woke me up in the middle of the night, resonating deep in my bones. Grace and ease—I'm still amazed at how good and right they feel. Immediately, I knew it was the trail I needed to follow. Over the next few days, I let the words *grace and ease* echo in my brain. They implied a way of living, a way of being. But how could I make grace and ease happen? Giving those words energy and force required turning them into some sort of conclusion. That's when I came up with the sentence, "It all turns out with grace and ease." Once I had that complete phrase I understood that grace and ease was a reminder for myself that I didn't have to work my tail off all the time or stress over every uncertainty: after all, it all turns out with grace and ease. Like a parent running frantically behind a child on a bicycle without training wheels, I learned that I could release my hand from the seat and let the bike go forward on its own. The balance, the speed, the whoops of delight followed.

Language Is the Access to Shifting Context

Our context is made up of our fundamental conclusions masquerading as reality . . . and since our behavior arises from those conclusions, if we want to have a different impact we have to shift the conclusions we are operating from. You can best think of the process by recalling the model that describes the DNA of context shifting that was presented as Figure 1.3. A revised version is presented here as Figure 3.1.

Figure 3.1 Redesigning Myself for Greater Impact

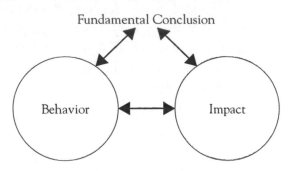

There is no exact right way to articulate your context. I strongly recommend that you put it in the form of a conclusion because that enables you to operate as if that is your new truth. Remember, you can use the context/bridge word/tail structure from Chapter One if it is helpful. The main thing is that you design a context that gives you freedom and power to lead yourself and others.

Some examples of successful new context designs from our clients include

> *OLD:* "I take charge so that I'm not left out."
> *NEW:* "Through relationships I'm a catalyst for greater leadership."

> *OLD:* "Taking up space in a group is not safe."
> *NEW:* "My peaceful power will ignite and contribute to others."

> *OLD:* "If I ask for help I will be exposed as not worthy."
> *NEW:* "My value comes from who I am, not just what I do."

For Gayle Dee, designing a new context was not simply a matter of focusing on the word potential. She needed to know how that potential was going to arise. Accordingly, she described herself with the conclusion that she was someone who revealed and helped fulfill potential in herself and others. You will need to make your own contextual phrase a conclusion, too.

Table 3.1 Design a New Context

Context	Bridge Word	Tail
_____	but	_____
_____	so	_____
_____	and	_____
_____	because	_____
_____	in order to	_____
_____	therefore	_____

Examples:

I speak up *because* my perspective adds value.

I am fiercely independent *and* I easily rely on others for my success.

I forge relationships *in order to* create better solutions.

The template provided in Table 3.1 can be used to explore language and design a new context.

Designing a new context is like building a three-legged stool. The most important leg to work on is the articulation of the new context. That is what we have done in this chapter. But that one leg must be supported by two other legs. The second leg is your behaviors—that's what we discuss in the next chapter, when we deal with Step 4, Sustain. The third leg is about creating the impact you desire in the world—that's discussed in Chapter Five, when we cover Step 5, Engage.

4

PRACTICE LEADS TO MASTERY

Step 4. Sustain Your New Context

Having daily practices allows my new context to gain momentum and sustainability.

Why SUSTAIN?

- Health, vitality, and resilience
- Collaborative partnerships
- Sustainable change with increased business results

Life shrinks or expands in proportion to one's courage.

—*Anaïs Nin*

Designing a new context is an exciting and exhilarating experience, but if you don't put it into practice, the changes won't stick. Absent any practices for sustaining your new context, it's folly to expect any lasting change.

You say you don't like practice? Well, you're already in practice every day. Your prevailing context—the one you've been operating from for years—is deeply embodied in your habits, thought patterns, and even your physical body. While you may not be aware of those practices, they are ruthlessly effective at keeping you stuck. With each passing day, you get better and better at perpetuating your old context at the expense of any new way of being, seeing, thinking, or behaving that you (or others) might prefer.

Practice, practice, practice. You've long heard the adage "Practice makes perfect." Well, I've never met a perfect person yet; but I do know that *practice makes permanent*. In order to undo the habits of a lifetime and reroute the well-trodden paths in your personality, you need to develop new practices that help sustain your new context. Think about the practice required to do scales on the piano, achieve balance and grace in a strenuous yoga pose, or learn how to control and steer a Jet Ski cutting through bouncing surf at 40 miles an hour. New muscles, new instincts, and new mental approaches are involved in operationalizing your new context and making it stick. Out of that work will come a new comfort with a new you.

It's critical to recognize that no change is sustainable if tackled in isolation. We are physical, emotional, intellectual, spiritual, and social beings. There is no such thing as changing one aspect of our lives and expecting everything else to fall into line. But there are levers and pressure points that we can pay attention to in order to make a shift. Context shifting is the ultimate extreme makeover in that it involves every aspect of your life. Therein lies the critical difference from other change efforts you've made over the years. You've probably tried a new diet or new exercise regimen before, or vowed to live differently or better—yet failed to see a lasting impact. No doubt, there have been moments in your career when you've experienced the disruption of a major organizational or team change effort, too—initiatives launched in grand fashion that ultimately failed to make a difference. Why?

As someone who has monitored a lot of change efforts over the years, I can tell you that there are two pitfalls to be wary about. On the one hand, when most people desire individual or organizational change, they tend to focus on behaviors, actions, or practices, without paying sufficient attention to the context in which those changes need to occur. In other words, failing to reveal, own, and design context means that desired behavior changes will be taking place only on the surface, without going deep enough to nourish long-term growth. On the other hand, there are some people who are good at designing a new context for the changes they seek, but they fail to support that trade-up with deliberate practices that will make the changes stick. In such case, the new context is like rich soil that lacks any grass or trees—soon drying up, eroding, and blowing away in the next strong wind.

In order to resolutely and sustainably change your life and career, you need the reliability of a three-legged stool that includes shifting your context, adopting new practices, and engaging in a leadership endeavor. In the previous chapter we looked at how to design your context. In this chapter we focus on how to adopt new supportive behaviors. In Chapter Five we look at shaping the impact you desire to have on the world.

Figure 4.1 The Process of Trading Up

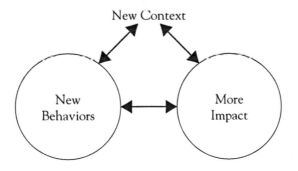

Throughout this journey, keep the DNA model of context shifting (presented here as Figure 4.1) in mind as a way of understanding the complicated dynamics of personal or group change.

From Leprechaun to Leader

How do your behaviors, attitude, and physical body have an impact on how you "be" in the world? To understand this better, let's look at Dr. Colleen Brophy.

Colleen Brophy is the national rock star of vascular surgery. She's Chief of Vascular Surgery at the VA Medical Center in Phoenix, a research professor of bioengineering at Arizona State University, and a clinical professor of surgery at the University of Arizona. Just in case you didn't think Colleen was busy enough, a few years ago she founded and led a start-up biotech company that developed an assortment of valuable drugs. (She sold off that company in 2006.) She's received a plethora of awards and research grants, serves as an editor on the *Journal of Surgical Research*, and has more than seventy publications in peer-reviewed journals. On top of everything else, Dr. Colleen Brophy is a dedicated mother to two very active daughters.

Colleen was born into a high-achieving family in Minnesota and grew up dissecting frogs on her mother's kitchen table. (Her sister and brother are both remarkably successful in the business world.) She moved to Utah when she was a sophomore in high school, and as an academically driven person, she didn't fit in very well in a place where most high school girls only aspired to getting their MRS degrees. A gifted female was supposed to hide the fact that she was intelligent. Colleen had maintained a 4.0 average without much effort, so she spent most of her time on the ski slopes. Her teachers told her mother she needed to do something about her daughter—so Colleen was sent to college early. The original Doogie Howser, Colleen started medical school at the University of Utah in Salt Lake City when she was just nineteen. She was one of eight women in a class with ninety-two men. Four years later, she moved to the east coast, a part of the country she'd never visited before, and became a surgical resident at Yale University School of Medicine.

Colleen was the youngest of the surgical interns. It was a trying though formative experience. "Residency was absolutely brutal," Colleen remembers. "The worst part of it was when another intern quit and I went five solid days and nights with no sleep. We were working 120-hour workweeks. They don't do that anymore [by national mandate, surgical residents cannot work more than eighty hours in a week], but while I was there I kept saying to myself, 'I'm going to survive this so I can change it.'" She went on to become a Vascular Fellow at Harvard University, served on the faculty at Yale University, and became Professor and Chief of Vascular Surgery at the Medical College of Georgia before moving to Arizona with her daughters.

Throughout those years, Colleen came to feel like a hamster madly spinning a wheel to go faster and faster. "It was all about achievement," Colleen says. "Achieve, achieve, achieve. But something was missing, and I felt that it was time to figure out what that was. Clearly, once I thought about it, I realized the missing piece was a higher purpose—achieving for the sake of what? I needed to figure out what I cared about, what I wanted to do and accomplish." The answer came quickly. As an insider who had seen the good, the bad, and the ugly of health care, Colleen had always longed to change the system dramatically. Now was the time, she realized, to do something about it rather than complain and criticize.

The problem, however, was that Colleen did not project leadership or command attention. Meeting her, you would not have suspected that she was consumed by a desire to transform health care, nor would you have imagined her possible of helping facilitate such a change. Despite everything she'd accomplished in her stellar career, Colleen kept such passions carefully under wraps. You couldn't hear the energy of her vision in her words and you couldn't see it in her body. Unlike many participants in our program, Colleen was satisfied with her personal life and had no pain point in any of her relationships that was driving her to change her behavior. Instead, Colleen wanted to change her impact on the world. Working backward from "impact," she did some very serious reflection on how her behaviors and context limited her results.

One of the first things you notice about Colleen's presence is her size. Small in stature, Colleen also has a strong tendency to stay in the background. Growing up, and in her early career, people did not notice Colleen until she did something brilliant or said something remarkable; then she would disappear again. This approach to life was so successful for her that she was able to identify it as her prevailing context. When she put that context into words, Colleen described herself as a leprechaun, an often invisible creature able to pop out of nowhere and perform magic.

Being a leprechaun had been a very comfortable and productive context for Colleen for many years. I believe it provided her a way to lower her visibility in a series of environments where she would otherwise have been a natural outcast or target while still allowing her to shine and excel. In Utah, being a leprechaun allowed Colleen to survive what could have been a stifling and hostile school experience. Later, when Colleen began her hospital work, her leprechaun context allowed her to function below the radar screen in a macho and abusive environment. As her career thrived, people recognized Colleen as a great administrator and a terrific surgeon, but they never felt threatened by her because they never considered her to be a leader. She kept her criticism of the system to herself while letting others push their ideas or agendas to the forefront.

Nevertheless, Colleen understood rationally that being the leprechaun wasn't a positive or influential persona from which to operate if she wanted to change the nature of health care, so she threw her tremendous energy into learning the art and science of context shifting. Colleen formulated a new context: "I'm a courageous leader with heart and vision." She believes that well-being is a birthright for every person in the world. In Colleen's view, achieving that goal means creating a context shift in the minds of doctors and patients. It's about rethinking how we promote good health and building a different kind of relationship between doctors and patients. While that sounds like an extraordinary task, the changes we need to make can be profoundly simple. As Colleen put it to me, "So much of what we treat surgically, for instance, we could heal by telling patients to walk twenty minutes a day. That's why America's health care service is the most expensive in the world." Colleen's passion is to ignite and convene people who share her vision to change health care and are willing to roll up their sleeves and do the hard work necessary to make a difference. This encourages her to engage with others more openly and purposefully in support of her cause.

It's no small trick to turn a diminutive leprechaun into a courageous leader, so Colleen needed to work on operationalizing her new context on a number of different levels. First of all, we noticed that physically Colleen embodied her leprechaun context by always standing back on her heels. In order to embody her new context, Colleen learned to roll forward from her heels to the balls of her feet, a posture that was a constant reminder of the more generative and direct role she wanted to take in pushing her cause. Now, whenever Colleen speaks, whether in a meeting, one on one, or in front of a large group of people, she makes herself consciously roll forward. That physical act reminded her of her new context and how much she wanted to have an impact through her presence and words.

Besides being a leprechaun, Colleen's objectives were thwarted by her pace of work, the way she let things consume her as she tried relentlessly to achieve specific objectives. She came to understand that trading up to a new context meant being more centered. She learned to slow down and breathe and be more present in the moment, whether that involved thinking through a problem clearly, talking with a patient or a colleague in a fully engaged way, or reaching out passionately to a group of interns in a speech about the opportunities they would have to make a difference. She gave herself permission to spend time nurturing her own physical health because she recognized, as a vascular surgeon, that taking care of herself was a productive way of sustaining her energy and reaching her goals. Finally, on another level, Colleen realized that it was necessary to give up her default "I can fix it" mentality. Not everything in life could be attacked directly and resolved immediately. In particular, transforming a behemoth like health care meant thinking about change in a quantum rather than a linear way. In other words, Colleen knew she could never transform health care single-handedly. Rather, by seeding change in many different places all the time, Colleen could create lasting ripples that would grow in strength and impact.

Strategically, and in a practical sense, Colleen began to assert her influence on a number of areas at once. Her first concern was the core culture surrounding the almost mythical figure of the doctor-surgeon. The surgeon, after all, is the epitome of medical skill as well as arrogance—an almost Godlike figure in the hospital. A surgeon does not need to explain his actions or decisions, and he is never questioned. Naturally, the relationship between patient and surgeon is rarely open and communicative. Surgeons hardly talk to their patients, let alone get to know them, and their relationships to medical staff are usually not much better. As Colleen puts it, "If we're trying to change this macho 'I am a solo combat warrior and the only one who can handle this' attitude in health care, surgery is a good place to start." Colleen noticed the effect that assuming the "macho, I can do anything, never be vulnerable" attitude had on her body. In addition to being back on her feet, her shoulders were drawn in. It was a physical way to protect her heart, her vulnerability. The act of pulling her chest up and out, as if someone pulled a bucket handle on her chest, was another somatic practice Colleen used. "The effect this had on the people around me was amazing, I was viewed as more approachable. I had never realized until I adopted this practice how much I missed by physically closing myself off."

As chief of vascular surgery at her hospital, Colleen is in a powerful position to impact the way doctors relate to patients and think about health. Through her guidance surgeons at her hospital now operate as a team—a rare approach in modern medicine—and no longer talk about such and such a patient as "my patient" but share caring through team responsibility. This helps them think about the goals of health care differently. "I try to engage doctors and show them that they can't fix everything with an operation," Colleen says. "We're trying to teach physicians to go below the head and use their heart and gut, to start paying more attention to patients in what they care about, and what they want. We are terrible about that in the health care profession. For instance, one of the absolute certainties about our existence on this planet is that we will all die. And yet this is one of the biggest things we are in denial about. We spend about 90 percent of our health care dollars on the last ten months of life. We are not good at addressing death as inevitability. Some of the best deaths I've had the opportunity to participate in have taken place when we've come to agreement with the family that we've done pretty much everything we should and they can be at peace with their loved one when they die."

The approach Colleen is using to try to transform health care is holistic in nature. As Colleen explains, "It has to do with research, with the way medicine is practiced in the hospitals, with the dialogue of politics, and with the way companies operate. But it has to start with who I am being as a surgeon, scientist, and most important, healer." On any given day, she'll be role-modeling for interns, talking to the chief of surgery at some world-class medical facility, or recruiting a major drug manufacturer to join the cause. "I am engaged," Colleen says, "and I keep it to a level that is containable and doable." As an example, Colleen cites her work with the American College of Surgeons, where she has led the Young Surgical Investigator Course for the surgical research committee. "We're very underrepresented with women and minorities, so I teach young surgical investigators how to get funded. I bring in people from the National Institutes of Health and the College of Surgeons, and we set up courses with a lot of role playing involved where young surgeons actually practice writing and reviewing grants. I enjoy giving my inspirational talk about doing the research for something you care about. It used to be about what disease you want to cure; and now it's moved to how do you want to promote the health of human beings. I want young surgeons to truly think about the impact they want to have, and to go for it."

Everyday Behaviors and Embodied Practices

From leprechaun to courageous leader. Reading about Colleen, you could be led to believe that such a transformation takes place easily, at the snap of the fingers. Don't kid yourself. The practices of our prevailing contexts are deeply encoded in who we are, how we perceive the world, and how we come across to others. Prevailing contexts do not get altered without an understanding of the dynamics of change and a strategy for sustaining it.

What motivates us to want to trade up? It seems as though the only thing that really inspires change is pain—the desire to stop doing something that is causing suffering through unintended consequences, or the frustration of not accomplishing something we desperately want. No matter where your pain point comes from, you can work backward from it to understand how to shift your context, and then forward again to learn how to adopt supportive new practices.

When I say *practices*, what do I mean? Practices in general can be divided into two broad categories. I call them (1) behaviors and (2) embodied practices.

Behaviors are those things you do or say as you maneuver your way through the world. They can be observed, recorded, and pointed out. A scientist at a zoo, an executive coach at a company, or a spouse or child are all experts at watching what others do, taking careful note, and sometimes drawing attention to those behaviors. We've all got behaviors that set us apart. Although those behaviors are volitional—things we *deliberately* do or say—we are fairly unaware of them because they are so ingrained in who we are and how we act. Fortunately, we have lots of people around us to point them out. *I hate it when you do that!* is usually the form in which such information gets imparted to us. In other words, although we undoubtedly engage in many behaviors that are not offensive, disturbing, disruptive, or irritating, it's the behaviors that get under other people's skin that end up driving a desire for change.

In my work at my company, for instance, I was noted for certain behaviors. I worked fourteen-hour days seven days a week. I was harried and busy much of the time. I went above and beyond the call of duty whenever a client had a need, and I never slowed down. Of course, I didn't really notice those behaviors on my own. In fact, I thought they were natural—the perfect and practically only response to whatever situation I found myself in. In truth, you could say those weren't behaviors that I produced, but behaviors that ran me, the way computer code runs an operating system. At the same time, they were also behaviors that were taking a distinct toll on my life and unintentionally causing suffering in the people around me.

Fortunately, some of those people pointed out my behaviors by providing me with *feedback*. As you've probably noticed in your own life, it's rare when people point out the good things you do; instead, we usually become aware of the things we do because of their unintended consequences and the collateral damage. I quickly understood that because those behaviors came so naturally, they were rooted deep, deep, deep inside me—and were in fact manifestations of my prevailing context. In other words, those behaviors gave me clues for revealing and articulating my prevailing context. Once I named that context—"I'll never get anywhere in life without my nose to the grindstone"—I was able to understand how big an impact that context was having on my way of operating and how far back in the past that context had been formed. Raised poor and scrappy as a child, I knew from my earliest days that I wouldn't get anywhere in life without my nose to the grindstone for the simple reason that it was true! Fortunately for me, nose to the grindstone was a successful belief that helped me attain a lot of wonderful things. Unfortunately, by the time I reached my fifties, the wheels on that express train had come off the rails, and I needed to find a new track for the future. In other words, I needed new behaviors going forward—and I couldn't successfully adopt those new behaviors without trading up from nose to the grindstone to a better, more useful context.

In addition to the behaviors I exhibited through nose to the grindstone, there were a number of embodied practices I exhibited, too. For many people, the term *embodied practices* is an unusual or abstract concept, but let me try to explain. If you picture the human personality as an onion, you can get some sense of how this fits together. On the surface, you've got behaviors that are observable—such as rushing around like crazy, being agitated and forceful, or driving others to work hard. Deep in the core of the onion is your prevailing context—your personal history and character—like nose to the grindstone defined me. In between the core and the surface are your embodied practices—you can think of them as innate expressions of your prevailing context that appear in your body like a flickering image on the surface of water.

Embodied practices straddle your inner and outer self, providing subtle clues to others about what really goes on inside you while also giving you a stance or position in which to meet and receive the world. For example, if you had a camera that could take a somatic picture of me in nose-to-the-grindstone mode you would be able to see a person who was always leaning forward, thrusting her body into the fray. The image is perhaps best described by visualizing someone actually putting their nose to the grindstone: concentrating on the work at hand, focusing energy with a fierce intensity, probably grimacing. No mistake, this was also a very generative and powerful posture. My energy inspired tremendous energy in others and generated wonderful creative sparks.

Compare my behaviors and embodied practices with Colleen Brophy's. When Colleen was in a meeting, she stayed quiet and rarely spoke up to contradict anyone or steer the group's agenda, unwilling to put herself forward as a target. Instead, she typically saved the things she wanted to say for afterward, outside the meeting, speaking one on one with a trusted colleague. In terms of her embodied practices, this tendency to be a wallflower manifested itself by her physical position. Unlike my leaning-forward pose,

Colleen tended to stand physically back on her heels as if pulling away from the frenzy in front of her.

If you're skeptical, you probably wonder whether the physical posture I'm describing really does indicate Colleen's inner state or has an impact on how she relates to the world. In fact, it's critical. *Embodiment* is a term that describes the causal connection between matter and mind or the physical body and the spirit or intellect. Descartes said, "I think, therefore I am," but most psychologists know that how and what we think—in essence who we are—are intrinsically connected to our physical body, our environment, and the way we were nurtured. In many cultures and societies, however, human beings have an aversion to the body, or at least a distinct lack of body awareness. I'm not saying that we don't know what our bodies look like, whether we have love handles or ugly feet, but I am saying that few of us understand our bodies in the manner that a professional athlete or a highly skilled karate or yoga practitioner does.

If we really want to sustain a context shift, we not only have to adopt new volitional behaviors, we also have to adopt new embodied practices. In this part of our process, we've integrated the work of Dr. Richard Strozzi-Heckler. Richard has made a lifelong study of leadership through the human body. "The body, in the somatic sense," Richard writes, "expresses our history, commitments, dignity, authenticity, identity, roles, moral strength, moods, and aspirations as a unique quality of aliveness we call the 'self.'" Transformation is not possible through a mere change in words, behaviors, or positive thinking—what's necessary is establishing a "series of recurrent practices of mind, emotion, language, and body."

Somatic awareness or consciousness of our embodied practices becomes more possible when we understand the impact of our prevailing context. In our workshops, we demonstrate the link between physical presence and inner state. Our work with the horses in the corral is predicated on this idea. Horses do not understand words, and they are only marginally interested in our behaviors. They are, however, highly attuned to our physical presence—our body language or embodied practices. Our energy is all the horses have to go on. The horse that won't move to our commands, or that drags us around the ring, or that poops upon hearing us speak is telling us precisely what others feel when they encounter our body language, too. Malcolm Gladwell, the author of *Blink: The Power of Thinking Without Thinking*, describes this kind of communication between dogs and their owners. As Gladwell writes in an excerpt of *Blink* that was printed in the *New Yorker*, "A dog cares, deeply, which way your body is leaning. Forward or backward? Forward can be seen as aggressive; backward—even a quarter of an inch—means nonthreatening. . . . Cock your head, even slightly, to the side, and a dog is disarmed. Look at him straight on and he'll read it like a red flag. Standing straight, with your shoulders squared, rather than slumped, can mean the difference between whether your dog obeys a command or ignores it. Breathing even and deeply—rather than holding your breath—can mean the difference between defusing a tense situation and igniting it" (May 22, 2006, pp. 135–136). Gladwell goes on to describe how much human personal presence influences dog behavior even when one dog meets another as their respective owners take them out for walks. According to Gladwell, behaviorists claim that one dog's reaction to another on the sidewalk has a great deal to do with the sizing up of the tension or emotional energy of each owner—a tight leash, a look of concern, or a pulling back motion can signal that aggression is an appropriate response to the strange dog.

Human beings are not immune to these signals in each other, even if we may receive those signals only on an intuitive or subconscious level. Yet, when we become attuned to such signals by being made aware of their existence, we can begin to see the messages that embodied practices articulate. For instance, the man with the caved-in posture views life as a trial and a burden, while the woman who is confident and centered stands tall without slouching. With practice, you can spend a day at the mall watching strangers go by and make good guesses about their prevailing contexts. To demonstrate in the workshop, we do some simple exercises. For instance, one person stands still, while another person walks toward her with a hand out. The responses of those standing still are always interesting. The gesture of walking forward with a hand out gets interpreted as a request. Some people recoil, as if to say, "Ugh, another request!" Other people block the raised hand, as though warding off a physical blow. Still others move toward the hand, accommodating the request as though it were the most important thing in the world. Naturally, as leaders, we get requests all the time. Take a second to consider how you react to a request in the office? Chances are you feel that you make measured, rational, objectives responses to each request, and you cannot for the life of you explain why people react the way they do as a result. Watching the physical postures of people responding to a request provides a different snapshot.

In truth, most of us are terrible communicators because we don't know how our body is speaking above, beyond, and beneath our words. This works in two directions. As a person in a position of leadership, we're unaware of how our body communicates to others. At the same time, we also miss the signals others give to us, because we are insensitive enough to focus only on their words and not on their body language. A direct report can be explaining an important point to us in a calm tone, all the while communicating the fact that they are afraid. A sharp response from us, insensitive to their fear, can cause them to shut down. As another example, we can innocently ask a question of someone who has a very combative prevailing context and be taken aback when an argument erupts. As you know, these types of misunderstandings happen all the time. Eighty to 90 percent of what we communicate is somatic, and only a fraction can be found in the actual words.

Becoming more sensitive to our own embodied practices leads us to adopt new ones. For Keith Hollihan, who worked with me on this book, getting in touch with the physical expression of his prevailing context came through insights in yoga. With two young children, a wife in graduate school, and bills to pay, Keith's default mode over the past several years had been "All work and no play." Despite curtailing much enjoyment in life, this mode felt right to him because it matched the puritanical sense of obligation and duty instilled by his parents, who had struggled out of impoverished upbringings.

When Keith looked for embodied practices that exhibited this context, he noticed one right away. For the past several years, he had been experiencing a slouch in his posture that was collapsing his chest and causing him physical discomfort. While this could be explained by poor sitting in front of the computer for long hours, it was also present when he stood or walked, creating the sense that there was an imbalance between his physical and intellectual selves or that his head was outweighing or dominating his body.

During the course of our writing work together, Keith began cycling again after a year's hiatus and decided to train for a grueling organized ride in the Sierra Mountains. As the date of the ride neared, there were many opportunities to find excuses to cancel his participation and avoid competing. For instance, the work of this book was intensifying and we had a publisher's deadline to meet! But I encouraged Keith to take part, and he was able to successfully complete the ride. The experience of taking time out from work and dedicating himself to a pleasurable physical endeavor helped Keith get back in touch with his physical being and the sense of fun he'd known as a young athlete, while giving him confidence that more balance was achievable.

Still, shortly after the ride, life got busy again and quickly overwhelmed his best efforts at keeping up his new exercise regimen. A family vacation, pressing work demands, and the unexpected death of his father-in-law threw everything into the vortex. The collapsed chest sensation returned. Knowing that correcting this particular embodied habit was critical to sustain his new context, Keith turned to yoga. He practiced chest-lifting exercises and backbends as a way of instilling a body memory of his new mode of thinking. Even after ten years of regular yoga practice, backbends had been difficult for Keith. The sense of turning himself backward and upside down brought about fear and anxiety. He now viewed the pose as a way of lifting his chest, getting more in touch with his physical side, and embracing uncertainty. That daily practice helps remind him of the context he is trying to sustain, and the memory of the pose exists in his body whether he is sitting in front of the computer or walking down the street.

For Colleen Brophy, rolling forward on the balls of her feet and opening her chest was a way of influencing her prevailing context. In fact, the gesture was such a critical lever in her contextual psyche that it did wonders to make her more direct and outspoken. It also reminded her physically that she needed to keep working on expressing—and sustaining—her new context all of the time. Similarly, when I traded up to my new context, "It all turns out with grace and ease," I needed new behaviors and new embodied practices. In some ways, the behaviors were the easiest to come up with—although they needed a lot of *practice* to make permanent. I slowed down, refrained from panic, listened more closely, and stopped myself before speaking. But without altering my embodied practices, those new behaviors would have been unlikely to stick. The embodied practice of my prevailing context was to lean forward. The new habit I tried very diligently to embody was to plant my rear end squarely on the chair. By keeping my sit-bones attached to the seat, I reminded myself to restrain my energy. In fact, as this centering posture became increasingly natural, the position began to do much of my context-shifting work for me, refining my energy and focusing it better, while calming me internally and easing the concerns of others.

Jeanie Bunker, whom we met in Chapter One, needed to do some work to restrain her energy also. If you remember, I described Jeanie as a firehose, someone who always comes at you in full force. One of the embodied practices we devised for Jeanie was to have her walk flat-footed to meetings. This forced her to slow her pace and calm her emotional state as she entered a room. Upon adopting this new habit, Jeanie found the response in others immediate and remarkable. No longer did she fly into meetings to disrupt the energy of the group. Her new approach also helped her exhibit her new behaviors. She listened more closely, interrupted less, took better notes. This wasn't easy, and Jeanie worked deliberately to support those behaviors in a number of interesting ways. For instance, she created her own notepaper with watermarks on the corner of each page giving her messages like, "Breathe"; "Trust feedback"; "For the sake of what. . . . " And she made it a practice to save five minutes at the end of every meeting to ask for feedback as to what was and wasn't working in the relationship or the task at hand. The people around her knew she was sincere in wanting this feedback, and they were helpful in providing it to her in a generous spirit.

The combination of embodied practices, new behaviors, and supportive feedback was of immense benefit to Jeanie in managing her context shift. It helped that she was an athlete and knew from personal experience that practice is necessary to create body memory and improve. The impact of a new approach fades quickly if it only impacts the mind; real change sticks in the body.

As I said previously, what we practice becomes permanent, so it is essential to be clear about what you need to start or stop practicing. One simple way to articulate changes in behaviors and habits is to make two lists using the following box.

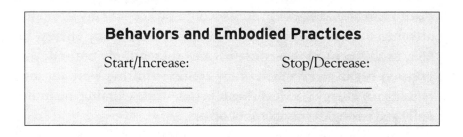

Behaviors and Embodied Practices

Start/Increase: Stop/Decrease:
_____   _____
_____   _____

Your Head Is a Bad Neighborhood; Don't Go in There Alone!

You start out with your new context in high hopes and with a sense of exciting adventure. As those feelings begin to fade, sustaining your new context becomes a journey fraught with dragons and traps—and none are so sinister as those perils you will encounter in your own mind. Let's talk about three of those dragons specifically.

"I still don't believe it." Once you return to the familiar surroundings of your everyday world, doubts begin to creep in. In the back of your mind you fear that your new context is a pretense, an act, a mask you put on. Sometimes this doubt is on the surface, sometimes it lurks another level or two down, whispering its message insistently. Let me assure you, this doubt is normal, but you need to shift beyond worrying whether your new context is real or not real. In fact, your new context is not a function of belief at all—it is a function of *practice*. In other words, your new context doesn't feel part of you until your embodied practices really sink in, and that only comes about through practice. By the time the doubt goes away, your context will have taken solid root. It all goes back to the calculus of competence and confidence we discussed in the previous chapter.

"I can't stop the voices in my head!" You know the committee—they're that gaggle of judges, skeptics, naysayers, boosters, cheerleaders, and suggestion makers who constantly chatter in your head. Some of the voices are positive and some are negative, some provide concrete and productive feedback, while others raise only doubts and suspicions that are without foundation. They wake us up in the morning, and they are still chattering as we try to fall asleep at night. Figure 4.2 shows a typical committee at work.

I remember the sound of my committee when my softball team went on strike and a new ownership group offered to buy the team on the condition that I serve as general manager. Some of the voices were congratulating me on being given such an opportunity. Other voices were saying, "Are you kidding? You don't know anything about running a team! You can barely balance your checkbook!" Then there was the voice of regret, letting me know that I would need to give up playing. And the voice of anxiety, informing me that my teammates would view the opportunity as a shameless power grab. In the end all of these voices could be reconciled and brought into line with a future that did not exclude the things I wanted

Figure 4.2 The Committee

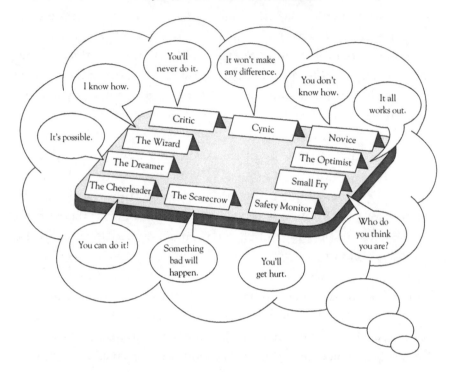

most, like being able to both play and manage. But if I had listened to any one of those voices too closely, I would have been swayed or diverted from the path I wanted to take. Each voice was reminding me of conclusions I had once lived by and was endeavoring to put behind me as I embarked on a new journey.

It will be easy, over the days and months of your new context shift, to drift back into old habits and thought patterns. Particularly in times of stress or threat, you will be quick to retreat to the inner sanctum of your head. This tendency never goes away. Although Colleen Brophy has become a master of context shifting, she still recognizes how much a role the committee plays. Describing a stressful meeting, Colleen said, "Oh yeah, the committee was screaming during that one." Listening to those voices would have been easy, but that would have meant reverting to her old context. We'll never be able to completely quiet those voices down. But one of the best ways you can bypass this ever-vigilant committee is to put your thoughts, emotions, and conclusions on loudspeaker with someone you trust.

"Nothing has changed." Look around and you'll see that's not true. Part of you is already operating under your new context and has been for some time. After all, you would never have come up with that context in the first place if it was not part of your personality at some level. Why haven't you noticed it operating before? Because such moments did not trigger any pain points or collateral damage. And why would they? It's only your old prevailing context that needed to be shed. You are not yet awake to the benefits that your new context produces. You need to draw your attention to those gifts consciously—and *register evidence* of them—as you grow comfortable in your new skin. For instance, when I began to adopt my new context, "It all turns out with grace and ease," I made it a habit to look for three things each day that came about with grace and ease. I also asked friends and colleagues to point out such instances for me. Together, we began to pick up on things that had never been on the radar screen before. They weren't hard to find, and the habit of looking for them made me realize that grace and ease was a growing part of my life.

The old context never goes away. It has brought you to where you are now. But adopting a new context can create new possibilities.

Just as you learn to register evidence of your new context taking hold, you also need to *celebrate your progress*. This doesn't have to be complicated. It can be silly, fun, or simply rewarding. Put smiley face stickers onto a grid whenever you catch yourself doing something right; give yourself permission to bask in the moment; throw yourself a party when you make an important decision or take a significant path that supports your new context rather than reverts to your old one. Believe me, you deserve it.

Self-Care and Centering

The other significant hurdle you will encounter is that your work of sustaining your new context takes place in the hurly-burly of life, when there are many other competing influences and demands beckoning for your attention, sapping your resources. You may wonder at times how you even stand a chance. All of the thoughtful calm, that poignant sense of the wholeness of life, the clarity of intention, and the authenticity you experienced when going through the reveal, own, and design steps of context shifting can dissolve in the frenetic vortex of the everyday.

The more you can slow down, get present in your own life, and practice the habits of reflection, the more available you can be as a leader for others. For Colleen, being conscious of moving forward on her feet also reminded her that she was "exactly where I need to be right now." Instead of listening to the committee of chatter-boxes in her head telling her all of the other things she should be doing, she was able to fully engage with the person she was with at the time. She also added the practice of walking more slowly and planting a smile on her face. Eventually, she had the patients at work engaged in supporting her in her new state. "Where is your smile, doc?" they would ask when she reverted to the tense, tight old context. She noticed that adding a smile changed her whole outlook. Psychologists have shown that smiling can actually change the way a person feels. Try it sometime!

Most of us have the desire to be more present, more in tune with our physical bodies, and more available to the people in our lives, but we lack a viable strategy for doing so. Commonly, we call this a desire for more balance. Despite all the efforts that have been made in corporate America over the past ten years, work/life balance is still the number one concern among employees. It's no wonder we have yet to resolve the issue. Most people's default context about work and life is that work and life involve scales that must balance like measuring weights. But since the belief that there is never enough time is a widely held conclusion, this context creates tension and hopelessness. There are, after all, only 86,400 seconds in a day and 525,600 minutes in a year. Within the default context of balance, your job becomes managing that time meter. By definition, this binary way of thinking reflects a sense of scarcity rather than abundance. Under such a rubric, engaging in work means subtracting from life, while engaging in life means taking time away from work. Nobody can win under such a system. It leaves us deprived and dissatisfied.

Moving from the idea of balance to the idea of "harmony" is one step that forward-thinking people are taking to better handle the issue of self-care. In this view, we are supposed to refrain from putting time into the equation and think instead in terms of quality and how well we manage to fit everything in. I propose taking that thinking one step further and viewing the idea of work and life as a harmonic in which who we are being and what we care about are brought into harmony no matter what activity we are engaged in. For instance, I worked hard at my company all last year but took a three-month sabbatical as well. One could view this as a binary split in my time—work offset by time off—but it never felt this way to me. Instead, I viewed my sabbatical as being in the service of my vision for my company and our customers, while also being in the service of taking care of me physically, mentally, and emotionally. During my sabbatical, I spent time with my daughter, played on my Jet Ski, attended a conference, vacationed with a close friend and colleague, and worked on this book. All were leisurely and productive uses of my time, and for someone who had long had her nose to the grindstone, my sabbatical was a demonstration to myself and a positive role modeling to others that I could indeed refrain from working like a dog until the day I die.

Taking Care of Others Doesn't Always Take Care of You

Leading others starts with leading yourself. Leading yourself starts with being responsible for your own well-being. It seems like a contradiction, but it's not. Let's think about the case of Susan Trainer as an example.

Susan Trainer has always been on the go, accomplishing more at a young age than many people could imagine in a lifetime. Her energy was quickly evident as soon as we got to know her. Despite the fact that she grew up around horses, Susan could not get the horse to slow down when she walked it around the ring. Were we surprised that she'd pulled up to the ranch driving a red Viper sports car?

Her parents were in their late forties when she was born; her brothers were eleven and thirteen years older than Susan. With such role models, Susan from her childhood had the mentality of an older person. She graduated from high school early and got her master's by the time she was twenty. By age twenty-one, she was working for a high-tech company managing a million-dollar research budget. By twenty-nine, she started her own communications firm and quickly grew it into a $4 million business working only with emerging high-tech start-ups. As an entrepreneur, hard work was wired into her brain, and she believed that she needed to prove her worth and capacity as CEO to her staff, clients, and venture capital partners every single day.

On top of this, Susan is married and has six children. After the birth of her fifth child, Susan's mother came to help her care for the children, then fell and broke her hip. Susan, on top of everything else, now had to look after her mother (who later developed cancer) and her children. As overwhelming as this must have been, Susan shouldered the burdens and kept plugging along, all while attempting to double her number of employees and grow her company.

As a leader, not to mention as a mother, wife, and daughter, Susan's default context was to take care of others. She called this being *Mama-sita*, or *Susan-sita*. This mode was particularly noticeable in her strategy for growing her company. In an industry with high turnover and at a time when skilled people were in high demand, Susan focused on "taking care" of her people. She made sure they were not missing vacations. She bought them birthday gifts. Instead of providing them with growth opportunities, she tried to buy their loyalty. At the same time, Susan was a micromanager. She felt obligated to check everyone's work. Most of that checking took place well after hours, after her own children were in bed and she was still sitting in front of the computer at one or two in the morning.

Susan felt stuck without really understanding why, and she believed the company was not moving forward. Susan's vice president and right-hand woman felt stuck too. To deal with her VP's dissatisfaction, Susan resorted to her default strategy. She figured if showing a little caring helped her junior employees, showing a lot of caring would help her most senior employee; so she bought her VP a new Volvo. On the day we were to begin working together, Susan's VP resigned to go and work with a client organization.

This crisis catalyzed a new context for Susan and her organization. Without her VP on board, Susan no longer had the physical capacity to oversee everyone's work. She'd reached a breaking point. In a highly emotional meeting, she asked for everyone to step up or step out. The quality of everyone's work had to increase. She worried that by informing her people that she was no longer going to be able to take care of them, and that she was demanding a higher standard, she would lose some if not many. Instead, the opposite happened. Her people were thrilled and excited. Several came up to her soon after and admitted they were set to resign because the workload was not challenging enough.

Through this experience, Susan received a valuable lesson on the difference between loyalty and commitment. She had loyalty down—it was a strength. But like many of us do with our strengths, she overplayed it and turned it into a weakness. When she understood that "taking care of others" was a default context for her, she could quickly see how it had come about. As a caretaker for so many other people, she secretly would have loved for someone to take care of her in a similar way. Unexpected gifts, roses for her birthday, a voice of concern for her threatened vacation plans—all would have been welcome. She misunderstood people's needs because she was not asking the right questions. "I was listening to words," Susan explains, "like *work, life, balance*. Those are serious words and you need to respect them. But I was talking with people who worked from home and did not truly have a work/life balance problem. What I did have was people who did not see their career paths, who did not see opportunity for growth, and who were a little bored."

Susan took ownership over the context she had set, under the presumption that "if it happens on your shift, you've got something to do with it." And she came to recognize that she needed to look after herself more and others less. "By no means am I there yet," Susan states, "but it's such an improvement. Getting my schedule down from sixty-five hours a week to fifty—that's huge in the life of a single mom with children. I've gone from taking care of people's personal lives and personal situations to providing people with career opportunity and growth. It came with the recognition that I am not that powerful, that I cannot make things okay for everybody, I can only give them opportunity. Ironically, they feel more respected as a result. Susan-sita, Mama-sita had to disappear for my organization to grow to scale."

Shutting Up Is a Good Thing

Susan's self-awareness came through crisis, but to maintain it and sustain it throughout a myriad of unpredictable situations, in the vortex of a growing company, a large family, and a wild economy, she needed to be present and centered, deliberate and intentional.

That capability starts, as my friend and coach Ellen Wingard has often said, with cultivating the still point. For most people, let alone most leaders, being still, taking time out for reflection, and engaging in deliberate practices that reduce one's exposure to the busy tasks of the day are difficult to manage and may even be considered inappropriate socially. And yet, nothing could be more important for maintaining a strong connection with our authenticity and our true intentions. As Ellen writes about the importance of centering:

> The quiet here is one of deep resolve that arises when we pause, breathe, and allow the noise levels of constant distractions and contradictory pulls to give way to a direct internal knowing. This quiet allows us to locate a sense of present-centered awareness from which we can observe and shift our habitual thinking to awaken

new perspectives. Here, we cultivate the "still point" where the tributaries of intellect, emotions, instincts, light, and shadow converge to reflect our core being. From this core, we are able to discern our own best counsel and give voice to wise solutions in the midst of seemingly insolvable daily complexity. The paradox of this quiet is that by pausing to reflect, we become more effective in the rigors of our day-to-day actions. (*Enlightened Power: How Women Are Transforming the Practice of Leadership*)

"Present-centered awareness" may be denigrated as a luxury in a world that prizes hectic activity and overwhelming commitment. And yet, there is evidence in clinical applications and recent neuro-scientific discoveries, not to mention ancient teachings such as yoga and Buddhism, that centering makes one more effective as a leader rather than less, by nourishing one's spirit, bringing health to the physical body, refreshing the mind, and inspiring creativity and inno-vative thinking. Richard Strozzi-Heckler, drawing on his research into Buddhism, Taoism, meditation, and aikido, writes that the state of being centered "produces the possibility of allowing the world in without being overwhelmed by it, and moving into the world with-out losing ourselves." It is characteristic, he describes, "in the person who embodies meaningful work and lasting relationships."

The more present a person becomes, the more open, percep-tive, and aware she is about her inner self, her work, and her rela-tionships. One of the default modes for most busy people, and again most leaders, is that they are always multitasking, doing many things at once, even two or three things that easily occupy nearly 100 percent of their attention. We talk on the cell phone as we drive. We answer e-mails on our BlackBerries in meetings or read documents on the computer screen as we talk on the phone. We make dinner and pay bills as we try to engage in quality time with our children. We work out while listening to an iPod and watching the closed-captioned news on a treadmill that's changing terrain over some virtual course. No wonder the quiet can seem deafening when it finally arrives. We are taking in so much of the world at such unrelenting force that the inner life becomes bottled up and closed off. We hardly know ourselves at first.

If we don't change that mode of being, then the work of sustaining a new context shift hardly stands a chance. So how do you physically go about "being centered" and engaging in more everyday reflection? It starts with new behaviors. We need to become aware that our ability to take on more and more and to overcommit and overdeliver, while a strength, is also part of the problem. Scheduling time away from commitments even while in the office is one very effective way many people manage to bring their lives under control. We need to refrain from engaging at times and resist those urges to always be in touch—checking e-mails before showering in the morning, getting on top of work on weekends, bringing the laptop along on vacations.

There are a number of ways you can build structure to your work of being centered. Some people take walks every day, first thing in the morning, at lunch, or at the end of the evening, using the time to attain a sense of connection with the self. Some people pray, while others meditate, practice breathing exercises, or engage in yoga. All are technologies for achieving stillness. Rather than self-absorption, these efforts make us more aware of what is going on. All of us have experienced the sensation of driving a car so absorbed by our own thoughts that we lose track of the miles that have passed. In fact, most of us live our lives that way, so locked out of the present that we don't experience what is actually going by around us. Through stillness and being present, you create an environment in which you and others can see what's really there. When you are preoccupied and not-present, you create a reflection of your own predetermined thoughts.

Design and Redesign

So here you are. You have become aware of your prevailing context, asserted ownership and responsibility for it, designed a new and better context, and developed sustaining practices leading to new supportive behaviors and embodied practices. Clearly, it's all over now. You're set. You will never have another problem again.

Of course, this is not true.

Trading up to a new context isn't an event, it's an ongoing process. As human beings, so long as we're alive, we do not get to rest. Don't worry, you'll get your time. We're all headed for the big nap. But until then, we will always have work to do. At any moment, even a new context that was generated or designed deliberately can become a default context. You will know that has happened when your new context loses some of its power.

When I settled on "It all turns out with grace and ease," I discovered a context that provided me with a wonderful opening and a perfect fit. Then I reached a point where I was backsliding into nose-to-the-grindstone mode. When I pondered why, I realized that I was no longer harmonizing with the way my new context was stated. I didn't know exactly why, but I could tell that I was creating too much stress and effort around me and my staff. After all they were a mirror of the leadership I was providing.

Not wanting to let the voices of the committee in my head rule my thinking, I put my worries on loudspeaker and sought out the counsel of two of my most trusted friends. This was done on the fly, in the middle of a major project, when I needed a boost to carry my team over the hill. Despite or perhaps because of the pressing sense of urgency, we quickly came up with a wonderful enhancement. My new context became, "It *always* turns out with grace and ease." Changing that one word pointed me in a new direction. It allowed me to see something from a new point of view. On the one hand, it served as an affirmation that grace and ease results. But it came with a caveat: I realized that if I didn't bring grace and ease into the equation, I wouldn't get grace and ease in return. This micronudge profoundly shifted who I was when I went back into the fray. It gave me a new vigilance and a new awareness of the ongoing role of my new context, even as it created amazing results in my business and relationships.

Trading up, like all growth in life, is a constant process. To use a music metaphor, there are peaks and crescendos. When you reach the rousing chorus, and all of the instruments are surging in harmony, you can ride that emotion and energy to great heights and distant places. During that time, you need to sustain that sense of direction and momentum through your practice and with the support of others around you. But it is inevitable that at some point the musical surge will recede, and your context will atrophy to become a default. It is then that you have to regenerate it.

You recognize that your context has gone stale when you are encountering pain points and generating unintended consequences and collateral damage. You use the techniques of context shifting to reengage with life on terms that are productive, fulfilling and meaningful. You grow, because growing is what we are meant to do. As B.K.S. Iyengar, one of the founders of modern yoga, has written: "Our flawed mechanisms of perception and thought are not a cause for grief (though they bring us grief), but an opportunity to evolve, for an internal evolution of consciousness that

---

Sustain Your Context

Activity: With a small group, brainstorm at least ten possible practices that will support your new context. Use Figure 4.3 to record them. Remember there are no incorrect answers. Welcome all ideas.

Figure 4.3

will also make possible in a sustainable form our aspirations toward what we call individual success and global progress."

All great performers, whether musicians or athletes, have practices that ensure they will be able to execute on demand. As you can see, leaders need practices too. In order to resolutely and sustainably change your life and career, you need the reliability of a three-legged stool that includes shifting your context, adopting new practices, and engaging in a leadership endeavor that requires you to operate from your new context in order to succeed. And with that we turn to Step 5, Engage.

5

TRAVERSING THE SPIRAL

Step 5. Engage Your New Context

Identify and Enlist Others
Engaging people to support my new context
allows it to become a reality.

Why ENGAGE?

• Shared purpose

• Optimization of everyone's contribution

• Enterprise-wide culture shifts

Our worst fear is not that we are inadequate;
our deepest fear is that we are powerful beyond
measure. It is our light, not our darkness that
most frightens us. We ask ourselves, "Who am I
to be brilliant, gorgeous, talented and fabulous?"
Actually, who are you not to be? You are a child of
God; your playing small doesn't serve the world.
　　　　　　　　　　　　　—Marianne Williamson

Life is a promise; fulfill it.

　　　　　　　　　　　　　—Mother Teresa

And now, it's time to connect with the world.

One of the things I see embodied very deeply in leaders is the tendency to become isolated. In many organizations, there's a good (or at least functional) reason for this trend. Executives often become highly political, emotionally cautious, and strategically calculated as they climb the monkey bars known as the org chart. Wary about being too open or increasingly separated by the bureaucracy of power, many leaders cut themselves off from friends and potential partners as they accrue responsibility. Even when such leaders confront one of life's pain points and realize the need for a big personal change—no small event in any successful person's life—they have a tendency to try to do all the fixing alone. No big surprise. The average leader has usually earned her tribal chieftain status because she is good at making things happen all by herself in the face of overwhelming odds. She thinks, "I've done it before, why not now? All I need is to put the old team back together—Me, Myself, and I—and we'll be all right."

If only it were true. Context shifts rarely take root in isolation. Context, after all, is a social phenomenon including everything and everyone around us. To place one booted foot in rushing water and hope to change the course of a river is folly. Eventually, you simply give in to the forces surrounding you and return to the overwhelming flow.

Yet, the temptation to keep your new context secret is very strong. Altering your perspective in such a transformative way places you in uncertain territory, a babe in the woods. It's as though, intellectually, you know that practice makes permanent, but you try to do as much of that practice as possible in the safety of your mind, avoiding the risk of going live. New committee members (the ones in your mind) are screaming in your ears, "You're going to look foolish when it doesn't work out! You're going to put your reputation, your career, and your relationships on the line!"

The problem, however, is that change does not get registered or become settled in the body unless it first begins to have impact in the world. If I had traded up to "grace and ease," for example, and never let anyone else know, I doubt I would have been able to tell when grace and ease was occurring around me. Nor would I have been able to spread grace and ease through my organization. Standing alone, locked into the transformations of my own mind, my efforts at trading up would have been the equivalent of leadership autism, full of sound and fury, signifying nothing.

Leadership in a vacuum is about as useful as lipstick on a pig. By engaging your context, you build a community of kindred spirits—people who believe this kind of transformative change is not only possible but imperative. It is through the support, reinforcement, feedback, and partnership of a community that you sustain your new practices and keep your context alive, while also sharing the capability for shifting context with the people around you.

The third leg of our three-legged stool requires us to engage in a leadership endeavor that will depend on our new context, new behaviors, and a community of partners for success. In this chapter I ask you to take on a groundbreaking project that will make a significant difference to your organization or community. In some ways this could be seen as a way of contributing value to your environment as you redesign yourself.

Enlisting Your Support Team

The first step, then, is to enlist your own support team. When we teach the methodology of context shifting to a group of committed leaders, the group itself takes on a life of its own. I have been amazed at the extent to which the participants stay in touch, arrange frequent gatherings, network with each other, build off each other's networks, listen to each other's challenges, and offer advice on shifting context on an ongoing basis. It is as though each person walks away from the event with a personal board of directors supervising the conglomerate of "me."

None of this occurs under my direction or suggestion—it just happens. And I think I know the reason. When you've come together with a group of strangers, shared your pain points, heard the common reactions to your private experiences, poked and prodded at your safest conclusions, dug up the deepest truths of your prevailing contexts, and undergone the exhilarating experience of trading up to a newly designed context—you feel connected in a unique way. The vulnerabilities you shared have drawn you close, and the energy you feel has made you excited about the possibilities for the future. Bouncing ideas off each other going forward is easier than with anyone else because you now have a deeply felt relationship and speak the same language.

It is more challenging but even more critical, perhaps, to engage with other nonbelievers back in the "real" world. First of all, the "old" influences around you are bound to be the strongest, and if you are not careful, they will pull you back into the past. At the same time, those old influences can be your closest, most helpful allies if you enlist them in your cause. And finally, the business of context shifting is not meant to be a solely self-focused or "me-driven" approach to life. It works best when it is accomplished through relationships, in conversation. A leader, after all, reveals and shifts context in himself and others. By enlisting others in your context-shifting efforts, you are working to help your supporters shift personal context, too. The impact of those efforts creates a better environment and a more expansive range of possibilities for everyone.

An important task, then, is to determine whose support you will need to sustain your new context. When I ask people such a question, the answers are usually self-evident. Frequently, there is a spouse or partner who comes to mind immediately. Next, there is often a close friend, or a group of close friends, who can be trusted. More creatively, there are usually a number of key figures in a person's life whose support is necessary in a variety of ways. Many of the top executives I've worked with have enlisted a key direct report or an administrative assistant. Often, such a person is able to provide a watchful eye and a helping hand in innumerable ways, from helping to shape a schedule that permits the openness and space needed for context shifting to letting the leader know how the impact of his work is registering—positively or negatively.

A final group, however, comprises those people whom you may not find it easy to approach or to solicit in your cause, but whose support would raise the quality of your environment and generate greater sense of possibility and creativity. Offhand, I can think of colleagues, peers, direct reports, and even customers who may be in competition with you for resources or status in your organization. There may be people in your family who fit that bill, too; or other relatives, neighbors, or friends; or people who serve or work with you at religious, school, or nonprofit organizations. It can feel very risky to engage such people in something so vulnerable as your change efforts—but the act of doing so can generate more surprises and more positive energy than you can imagine. Gretchen McCoy's story in Chapter Two of reaching out to her peers in a subdivision of her company provides an excellent example of how necessary and how fruitful such efforts can be.

Everything Happens Through Conversations

How do you engage others to support your new context and practices? Everything happens in conversation. Before enlisting someone, take time to consider the personality and character of the person you are trying to reach. You've probably seen him or her from a very limited or stingy perspective before. Open your heart and your brain to perceive him from his own viewpoint. What context is she operating from? How has that bumped into or interfered with your old context over the years, preventing you from getting closer? Most important, consider how your new context will match his interests or address his concerns, and be upfront about what kind of support you are seeking. Usually, we interact with people based on our level of trust. The people we relate to the deepest have earned our trust over the years. But what would happen if we just granted trust rather than requiring a person in a lesser relationship to earn it? We all have doubts about others, but context shifting requires us to suspend those doubts. Give your new partner the benefit of your sincere trust and compassion.

Whether you frame your conversation as a proposal, request, promise, offer, or invitation, a compelling context-shifting conversation is one that engages your partner and doesn't make him or her feel as though he or she is sacrificing anything to support you or join your cause. People respond positively when your conversation connects to their commitments and concerns. When someone says "No," it may only mean that they don't see the value in what you are laying out. By changing the context of the discussion and expanding the scope to include your partner's concerns and commitments, you are being a leader. The narrowness or expansiveness of a leader's context will affect all the people around them. If your scope is too small, it could limit the scope of other people's interests and dreams and your achievements together, putting a lid on everyone's energy, enthusiasm, creativity, and commitment. The key to expanding your context is making the choice to do so. Remember, as a leader you are in the context-shifting business.

Talk Isn't Cheap

In the left-hand column of Figure 5.1 are the five speech acts that produce action. Notice how things move forward if you say, "I propose that we . . . ," "I offer to . . . ," "I invite you to . . . ," "I request that you . . .," "I promise to. . . ." But you must be specific. For example, to whom are you making the request? What specifically

Figure 5.1   Action Conversations

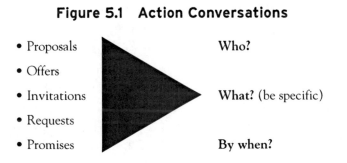

- Proposals
- Offers
- Invitations
- Requests
- Promises

Who?

What? (be specific)

By when?

do you want from that person? By when do you need him to fulfill your request? Most conversations without this level of rigor fall into the category I call "Let's do lunch."

Always solicit a specific response:

- Accept
- Decline
- Counteroffer

Building Relationships Expands What You Can Accomplish

The foundation of anything you and your partners build together is your relationship. Although we lead busy lives and have very pressing concerns, there's always enough time for relationship building. Whether you are enlisting people to support your context shift or contribute to your cause (and sometimes the two are intrinsically linked), you are working at building relationships in order to generate a new future and commitment. Dive deep into your own willingness to be at risk. Disclose as much as you can about your concerns and fears. The depth of your relationship is correlated to your level of generosity and your level of self-disclosure; and there is another direct correlation between how deep your relationship grows and how much value gets generated by it.

In Figure 5.2, the left-hand figure represents the correlation of what you can accomplish when you have one strong relationship, while the right-hand figure clearly shows the larger accomplishment created by many strong relationships. Communicated commitments and concerns are the bricks and mortar of relationship.

Don't let any conversation end without making sure your partner got what she wanted and needed. Go forward after knowing that you're both committed human beings who have connected in

Figure 5.2   Relationship Is the Foundation of Accomplishment

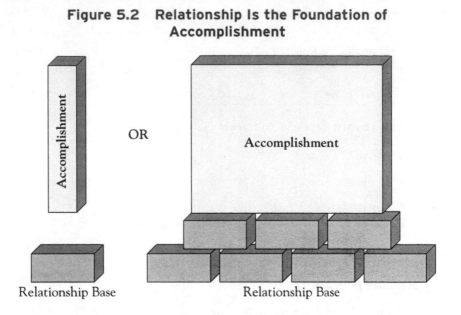

some significant way and want some of the same things in life to happen. How can you be afraid of such a person after that?

How Big Is Your Playing Field?

Engaging your new context means connecting with the world. But what is the purpose or objective that guides you in directing the impact you want to have? In determining your reason to lead, remember that critical question: "For the sake of what?" Think of your life as a giant magnetic field in which you get to play and work. How big is it? What does it attract and repel? Think of it as your purpose for living. How would you assess the size of life you have?

Most of us, imprisoned by prevailing contexts and hard-pressed by a multitude of ongoing concerns, can't answer "For the sake of what?" in any enlightened or expansive way. Caught up in the lane changes and traffic jams of the day to day, we lead what I like to call a drive-by life, barely able to see the dashboard, let alone the road ahead. Sometimes, it's only by examining the impact we're having that we can tell whether we're living in a helpful context or a diminished one.

Sometimes it is useful to start with an outcome or impact that you would like to produce. Figure 5.3 can help you to think through what impact you'd like to produce. If you work backward from that impact, you will see that it is going to be produced through action, and by now we know that your actions are derived from your context. But this begs the question, "Is individual action going to be sufficient to achieve this impact or am I going to need to scale up to the level of organizational action?"

Context shifting is about being able to change perspectives with agility, viewing life's fullness, nuance, and significance from a variety of angles and levels at once. As an illustration of what I'm talking about, think of a room in your house or office that's filled with plants. Some days you notice the plants, some days you don't. Mostly, they're just there. But plants are alive, and they interact with their environment in subtle ways that we rarely take time to observe. A forest stirring and swaying in an unseen breeze might remind you of the idea that all the plants within it are connected in some extraordinary way, sharing earth, air, light, and rain water, their leaves and roots intertwined. It doesn't take much to leap from that idea to imagining the entire planet breathing and

Figure 5.3   Desired Impact

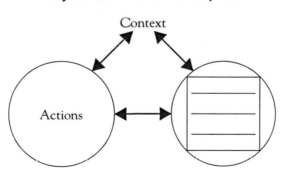

undulating with life. Now consider a plant cell on a slide under a microscope, and picture how different an impression you'd get of what a plant is. Better yet, take four microscopes, one that magnifies the plant cell slide by 5×, the other by 10×, the third by 25×, and the fourth through an electron microscope focusing on the plant cell at 100× magnification. Each microscope depicts an entirely different view of reality, the plant itself a world of darting shapes and circulating liquid. If a different person viewed the plant from each perspective—room, forest, planet, and the four levels of magnification—imagine the utter discrepancies that would surface if each observer began to describe what a plant looks like, how it functions in its environment, even how it stirs one in a poetic or spiritual sense.

Imagine your life in a similar way. At one level you are a parent, at another level you are a manager, at other levels you are a friend, sibling, and child. You may be a shareholder, an innovator, and a contributor to the community. You are certainly a human body, made up of cells, spirit, and intelligence, as well as a social being with relatives, friends, neighbors, and colleagues. You have a life with a history and a future of some undetermined length. You are many selves, some of which you have awareness about, some of which you hardly ever consider. Imagine, now, that you are able to focus and direct more of the energy composing those selves to some cause or objective that really matters? *For the sake of what . . .*

The Spiral

Everything we do in life can be connected to a larger impact if we think of it in terms of a spiral. There are at least five scales on this spiral that we all belong to: individual, team/group, organization, community, and society. For example, when you do a mundane task in the office, how can you connect that task to a larger purpose? Chances are, even the most unnecessary meeting or trivial report contributes to something larger than itself.

Creating the Line of Sight

The work you are doing may seem small sometimes, but extend outward and watch what happens as the rings spread progressively wider in impact. (See Figure 5.4.) At the level of the team, what is the contribution or impact you are making? At the level of organization, do you have an even bigger impact? What are the impacts at the levels of community and society? You can also connect to something more intimate and precious. How does your work influence who you be in your family? How does it impact your daughter's life? How does it impact your health and spirit?

Reality is a function of what we perceive at a given scale and at a given moment in time. For example, is the book you are reading right now solid? Answer again while viewing it under an electron microscope. . . . Clearly it would not be solid at that scale

Figure 5.4   The Line of Sight Spiral

Society

Community

Organization

Team/Group

You

of observation. The spiral helps you to adjust the scale of your thinking and connect everything you do to your greater purpose (*for the sake of what...*). The parable goes, a wealthy merchant was walking through a medieval town and stopped to talk to three workers laying bricks. He asked the first worker what he was doing, and the worker replied, "I'm laying bricks." He asked the second worker, and was told, "I'm building an archway." He asked the third worker, and was told, "Why, sir, I'm building a cathedral." If your spiral grows out of your authentic passion, then everything you do can be directed toward building your cathedral. It's a matter of recognizing that perspective depends on scale and time.

Shifting from Individual to Enterprise Context

A few years ago, for instance, a woman who was head of training and development for a huge Fortune 20 company came into a better understanding of the spiral and used it to improve the impact of things she cares about. Listening to my presentation, she told me, "I realize that I'm going to have a very different conversation with the CEO tomorrow than what I would have had." The next session, she reported to the group that the CEO had given her thirty minutes of his time to get through a PowerPoint presentation of the organization's training strategy, "but he ended up spending two hours with me." Now, CEOs of Fortune 20 companies don't have two hours just laying around, so I asked my client what she did to encourage her CEO to give her that extra hour and a half. She answered, "I did what you talked about. I scaled up to the level of enterprise and talked to him as a peer or colleague. From there, we started talking about our workforce strategy for the next ten years. I didn't focus down on a specific program or initiative. I scaled up the spiral and spoke from a different context." In other words, the spiral provided my client with a way of communicating at a new level of impact. She could have stayed locked into her context of training director. Instead, she went into the conversation with her CEO thinking, "Who would I be at the scale of corporate leader?"

Nancy Nelson is another client who brings this sense of scale to her thinking on a continual basis in order to magnify her impact. She's one of the kindest, most generous people you'll ever meet. If you saw her in a crowd, however, you wouldn't think of her as an impactful leader. She's not a showboat who dazzles; she is very understated even as she is bright, thoughtful, and consumed by a desire to make a difference, particularly for girls and women in science and engineering.

In her career, Nancy is a general manager in the engineering and construction group of Trimble Navigation, the company that pioneered GPS technology. As an electrical engineer, scaling up and out wasn't something Nancy was accustomed to: "All of my education from my engineering and early technical days was focused on the details, looking at only one thing, putting it under the microscope." This myopia left Nancy feeling wanting. "I was in crisis in terms of what to do with my life," Nancy admits. "Wondering where I belonged in my company and what I wanted to do." On the one hand, she was and is very successful at her work, managing a $30 million business to profitability and founding and running a successful nonprofit foundation. Nevertheless, while Nancy understood that she was making a social contribution in her nonprofit work, she saw little impact in her professional work, and the two sides of her life felt disjointed. As Nancy puts it, "I just never felt as though I was doing something that really mattered, or that it was important in the bigger sense. I knew we were doing innovative things in the company, for example, but I never thought about how it was impacting the rest of the world."

When she worked with us, Nancy came to understand the power of the spiral as a way of connecting her desire for impact to the work she was doing on a constant basis. She says that she now spends a good part of her day looking at the details of whatever she is doing from a variety of angles, being actively conscious of the impact she wants to have at each level of the spiral.

In her group's early work with the GPS technology, this way of thinking proved to be transformative. At first, GPS technology was considered just another electronic tool for navigation, without any particular applications. Today, a GPS operating system is thought about more like a computer—a powerful device that can be used to do a variety of important things. You can use it for navigation, timing, or positioning, and those functions can have a lot of value. To unearth those applications, Nancy and her group made it a constant practice to engage with the customer and think about the customer's needs. The context they embodied was one of constantly declaring, "What we are doing here is making a difference. It really does matter."

One of the early adoptions was particularly noteworthy. Nancy's group integrated radio technology with GPS technology for use on tractors in farms in California. This allowed the tractors to operate with incredible precision in plowing fields, resulting in a better, more efficient job. As a result of this innovation, crops could be planted over the course of longer hours, even late at night during busy season. The impact of this went beyond efficiency and productivity, however, extending to personal safety and health, since farmers working in the dark had frequently experienced accidents before the system was put in place. And there was an environmental impact as well, in the sustainability of resources, since the precision plowing allowed drip water systems so that less water was needed—a precious commodity in California and Arizona—and less chemical fertilizer, too.

"It was just incredible," Nancy says, "when we started to see this technology impacting the community and the environment. And we were saving people's lives. I was able to say to my group, 'Look at this, this is really good stuff we are doing.'" They started with a goal to make sure that the work made a difference and really mattered. Expanding outward from that central point along the spiral, they were able to show the impact of their work on larger and larger realms. Communicating that within the team, within the company, and to customers brought new energy in terms of connection, community, and innovation. "From there," Nancy says, "we were able to grow larger teams focused on new applications doing something that made a difference."

Meanwhile, Nancy was bringing contextual thinking to her nonprofit work also. Fourteen years earlier, she had founded a program within the Society of Women Engineers called GetSET (Get Science Engineering Technology). "The program," Nancy says, "is designed for young women starting high school who are part of underrepresented ethnic groups. Today, fewer than 20 percent of engineers are women. Very few of those women are African American or Latinas. Our program is built to attract young women when they are freshmen, and we bring them along until they graduate from high school." Nancy noticed a spiral-like payoff immediately. "Our first graduating class was 1996. The students who had graduated were really won over to engineering and science. Together with their moms, they started recruiting their cousins, sisters, and friends, and we became a small community. Some of the graduates came back as counselors. Being part of a community helped the girls see, 'I can do this.'" Through that support, the GetSET program made engineering an exciting option for hundreds of young women.

Nancy recognizes that context shifting has a diluted or diminished impact in isolation but thrives and grows in community. "The message we always keep in mind is, What you are working on does make a difference in the world. You just need to follow the spiral—look at what you do to make a difference, then look at what the customer does with your product to make a difference, and keep on going all the way out. By the time you've extended just a few levels, it's incredible the impact you can see. You begin to understand how everything folds together and you have a sense that what you do is not an isolated event."

The Power of Individuals to Create the Ripple Effect

As human beings, we are linear thinkers, focused on cause and effect. We can't easily see the branching and spreading that takes place whenever we take action in the world. But consider how ideas form in your brain. You never come up with a new idea when you focus on one specific issue and concentrate with all your might. Instead, your brain begins to wander and spark. Thoughts get chased down seemingly useless pathways. They connect, disperse, reconnect, until dozens of ideas are racing along, then *poof*, the idea you were seeking emerges in the front part of your brain. To believe that this idea was derived in a linear fashion is foolish; yet we dismiss the seemingly random activity of the brain as a distraction or lack of concentration from which the idea was plucked in spite of this detriment. As another example, consider a crowd of people watching a sports event in a stadium. Each person is an individual, with their own thoughts, reactions, emotions, and physical sensations, yet the crowd can also act as one—surging into emotional pitch when something exciting happens, sensing the mood like electricity, each individual rising to her feet or cheering when a point is scored as if wired to the same nervous system.

In fact, all systems exhibit this interconnectedness. When we consider the impact we want to have on the world we need to keep this in mind: doing something, anything, with intentionality *does* have an effect, even if we can't always predict where or how that effect will hit. Instead, our impact ripples outward, setting others into motion, too.

Leaders create fields of play in which other people collaborate. As a leader, ask yourself what size field you want to create. On the other side of the coin, consider whether you have been constrained within someone else's field. Deep despair comes from having so much to give and nowhere to give it. When you have a compelling vision of the future, you can't bear the reality of playing too small. Quite often in organizations, people come to work with big feelings and are forced to play on a puny playing field. If your field is vast, if it includes goals larger than those achieved in the past, your team will be inspired to accomplish the extraordinary.

In 1954, it was an absolutely unequivocal medical certainty that a human being could not run a mile in less than four minutes. It was a matter of anatomy, the experts said, a physiological impossibility. This conclusion set itself in the mind of the public to such an extent that the media referred to the barrier as the "miracle mile." Roger Bannister, a young medical student, decided to ignore twenty years of restricted playing field and prepared himself to break the barrier by dividing the mile into four segments and running each segment fast enough to beat the record if the segments were run continuously. On May 6, 1954, Bannister ran a mile race in front of three thousand people. Breaking the record proved the twenty-year conclusion was false, the playing field too small. Not surprisingly, however, once that playing field had been expanded, others were able to follow Bannister's path. Indeed, only two months later, Bannister's rival, John Landry of Australia, broke the four-minute mile himself.

Holding your passion and purpose close to the vest does little to help you realize your larger goals. When you are deliberate about what you want to accomplish, express your reason for leading, are engaged with people who can support you and your cause and conscious of the larger impact of your work, you can achieve groundbreaking results.

Shifting Organizational Context

In 1987, Anne Firth Murray established the Global Fund for Women in San Francisco as a small philanthropic organization that would raise funds and make grants to promote women's human rights and development around the world. Anne believed that not all money was the same color green. She felt that both the way money was raised and the method used for grant making were critical to creating sustainable impact. Rather than relying solely on large institutional donors that tended to have impersonal relationships to recipients, the Global Fund aimed to create a vast and diverse community of donors and recipients from a wide variety of backgrounds, income levels, and parts of the world. For instance, most funds and philanthropies rank individual donors by the amount of money they bring to the table; but the Global Fund does not classify or list donors by the amount given. Everyone who participates is valued as an equal partner. The grant-making model is also radical. The Global Fund gives general support to women's groups, trusting that they know best the solutions needed to make change in their communities. It puts critical decision-making power into the hands of those who have experience on the ground by inviting activists and former or current grantees from outside the United States to serve as advisors and board members of the Global Fund. In addition, in Anne's view, the organization's culture itself was an equally critical component in changing the model of mainstream philanthropy. She built, as she puts it, a "generous organization, that would work evenhandedly with women's groups around the world, with donors and volunteers, with staff and with others." It was her belief that changing the world meant changing the way people treat each other, and if the Global Fund modeled such behaviors internally, it would be able to forge such relationships in its donor-recipient community. I call that an innate understanding and application of the way the spiral works.

Raising money for international women's causes was not easy, however. Although the Global Fund did tremendous work, it operated on a yearly budget and relied on annual giving on an ongoing basis. Anne served as president until retiring in 1996, when Kavita Ramdas took over. Kavita was born in India but had lived in the United States since college. She did graduate work at Princeton, after which she worked in a number of non-profit organizations, such as the MacArthur Foundation, before joining the Global Fund—an organization with a very different model of philanthropy. She comes from an illustrious family with a famous father who was head of the Indian Navy before becoming a peace activist. She speaks six languages (three fluently) and is married to a man from Pakistan—no small issue in South Asia where the two countries, India and Pakistan, have gone to war three times. When you meet her, you are immediately conscious that Kavita is a citizen of the world and an articulate and enthusiastic leader and spokesperson for some of the most vital issues our planet faces.

Kavita came to our program at a time when she was trying to do some context shifting for the Global Fund. The organization had accomplished great things in its context as "innovative start-up," but in order to have a more lasting and profound impact on women around the world, people needed to know the Global Fund was going to be a "stable high-impact player." It was a message, as Kavita says, that "we are not going anywhere. We are going to be around for the long term, and you can count on us to be there for women, now and into the foreseeable future." She decided, as a practical application of this new context, that it was necessary to raise enough money to create a permanent endowment for the organization. In terms of her leadership, however, Kavita also recognized that it was critical to retain the values and culture of respect and community set in place by Anne Firth Murray, even as the Global Fund expanded its size and capacity many times over. To some leaders this would have been an either/or kind of decision point, with respect and community sacrificed on the altar of size, or ambitions restricted by a need to be true to the values. Instead, Kavita was able to expand the playing field to accommodate both priorities. Her spiral was centered on the values of the organization even as it grew to reach new levels of impact.

Over the next few years, each potential setback to the world of philanthropy became a new catalyst in Kavita's groundbreaking project. The first setback occurred in the immediate aftermath of the 2000 presidential election. Twenty-four hours after assuming office, the Bush administration issued the so-called global gag order. This meant that no provider of health services that receives U.S. government funding could even mention abortion in its work. Furthermore, the U.S. government rescinded its support to the United Nations Fund for Population Activities. As Kavita notes, this had a huge impact on health care providers working in the developing world. Suddenly, a myriad of nongovernmental and nonprofit organizations that had relied on U.S. government funding needed to find another source. Kavita says, "Even though we were such a small foundation, we became overwhelmed with requests. Women around the world were saying, 'We need you. We need you to step up.' And they needed confidence in our long-term stability." Compounding this crisis was another setback: the stock market crash and global recession of 2000. After seven years of exponential growth in wealth, and a corresponding growth in donor giving, the philanthropic community was hit by the worst economy in fifty years.

Then came September 11, 2001. In the subsequent focus on Afghanistan and the repressive rule of the Taliban regime, people began to see the link between our fortunes at home and the plight of women all over the world. "We had been working with women in Afghanistan for five years before 9/11," Kavita says. "We had known what was going on, and suddenly there was recognition that the liberation of women, and women's human rights, really do matter."

It was in this environment that the Global Fund launched what was originally an endowment campaign to raise $20 million. Its profile and sense of mission galvanized, the organization subsequently raised $10 million for its primary endowment. Meanwhile, the Iraq war began, and the leadership at the Global Fund and its community of women's groups in the Middle East were highly concerned by how the war would impact women in terms of increased violence and economic and social displacement. Despite the fact that the campaign was already underway, the board and staff decided that the current crisis required a response from the Global Fund consistent with its commitment to women worldwide. In midstream, it changed the campaign by adding a second fund, called the Now or Never Fund. Ten million dollars of the total raised by the IWC would now go directly to support women resisting militarization and war, rising fundamentalism, and attacks on their reproductive rights. Instead of falling into the binary context of *either* we can stay the course on our endowment fundraising campaign *or* we can postpone it and immediately focus on the urgency of raising funds for women in war-torn situations, the Global Fund enlisted its staff and donors in contributing to both efforts. Donors responded enthusiastically, and the Global Fund was successful in meeting all of its goals.

The Global Fund had come to embrace a size and capacity that would have seemed impossible under its original context of "innovative start-up." During this transition and activity, Kavita says, "There were moments when we had a really tough time and started questioning our goals. In particular, I really needed to look at my whole management style and leadership approach." Kavita found that the practice of context shifting supported her leadership goals, however. The organization had always operated on the principle that local women's groups are the best judges of what they need in their own local communities. But in response to the fund's new mission to advocate for women's rights at a higher level, it expanded its role to include support networks. As Kavita puts it, "Women want to have their voices heard on multiple levels."

Despite this broadened role, the importance of listening critical in leaders working to reveal and shift context in others— was reemphasized for Kavita. "Listening to women, allowing them to speak in their own voices, uncovering what their priorities are has been critical for our work. As you grow larger, it can be difficult to keep the commitment to do that, but we knew it was our key philosophical commitment. What I found so interesting is that the vehicle for doing so is good leadership practice. [Contextual leadership] is not just a nice thing to do—it actually results in good outcomes. That was an *Aha!* for me."

As the organization has grown in size and struggled to an extent with its own success, there is nostalgia for a simpler time but an understanding of the benefits of enlarging the playing field. "Investing, growing the organization (sounds disrespectful to the past—it was always something!), going from a volunteer office with one or two people to a thirty-eight-person office where we are always welcoming newcomers but don't always recognize every face anymore … yet there are so many things that would not have been possible if the Global Fund was not big enough. We're now awarding over five hundred grants a year worth almost

$8 million to over three thousand groups in 162 countries. Our annual grant-making budget makes us the largest independent funding organization for women in the world. And our individual donors have reached twelve thousand in number in 2006." Kavita continues, "I dream about manifesting in a small organization the kind of world where people respect the dignity of others, where diversity is valued, where there is time for listening, and time for individual relationships. And I think those values continue to inform the work of the Global Fund. I do not mean to be hopelessly idealistic, but I think you'll never get the outcome you want until you can visualize the kind of world you want and work to bring it into being. We want to change the context of profit, to shift from a narrow definition of the monetary bottom line. For business to be good, business has to do good, and the notion of profit must include profiting by making good friends, taking care of the health, spirituality, and well-being of the Earth, and doing things that are worth doing."

Following the spiral and expanding her playing field has allowed Kavita to think about leadership in entirely new realms of impact. As a context shifter, she has seen the effect of this work on herself, her organization, and around the world.

Create Your Own Groundbreaking Project

I advise everyone who learns the five-step process of context shifting to put it into practice, not just in her own life, but in some critical aspect of her work as well. Organizing your context-shifting work around a key objective gives you the drive, stamina, and—frankly—the courage to engage all of your new muscles at once. This takes you out of the realm of the safely theoretical and into the arena of the real world. The setbacks you meet need to be dealt with in real time. Lacking all the necessary resources, you seek out people who can help. In each encounter and relationship, you are actively aware of the contexts at play and are working to shift them. It's an exhilarating experience and does wonders to settle your new context into your body and practices.

A Few Committed Women Change the
Future of Australia

In 2001, I was asked by Anne Skipper to partner with her in con-vening a luncheon in Australia to a group of fourteen women from all sectors that included several high-ranking officials in public agencies. My definition of a leader is one who speaks for, listens for, and evokes action on behalf of a compelling future. So part of the challenge that I put to these leaders was, "What future do you want to help create?" During our discussion about what each wanted to accomplish, both in their personal lives as well as with their work, one of the participants mentioned that she would like to see more women in political positions of national importance, such as the prime minister's appointed cabinet positions. "Well, how many have you got now?" I asked. "None," was the response. As it turned out, in the *entire* history of the Australian Commonwealth—more than one hundred years of government—only *one* woman had ever served in a cabinet position during any given administration. I was shocked. The more we talked, the more certain these leaders became that opening up the old boys' club of policy making was the goal for which they were willing to enlist as leaders. I saw it as an opportu-nity for them to put their context-shifting skills into action.

Their game plan came together over the next two months. First, we established a network and sought to actively expand the spiral. Each leader pulled contacts from her Rolodex—including journalists, government officials, public agency leaders—with whom they could have context-shifting conversations about getting more women into appointed national positions. Their list of talking points included names of other women who had the experience to be viable candidates for those slots. The lead-ers decided to call their effort "Five in Five." In other words, they hoped to have five more women in appointed positions as a result of the group's efforts within five years.

One leader striving to make an impact on the world is one thing, but a group of leaders, mutually enthusiastic about a cause, and applying their efforts through their own networks, was truly something to behold. A major metropolitan daily newspaper, for instance, ran a story about the lack of women in government. Another story, in another publication, profiled the "Five in Five" effort. Within six months, the group had elevated the visibility of the issue of women in government in the public, as well as in political circles, to the point where it could no longer be ignored. In other words, they shifted the conversation going on in the public about politics and changed people's perspectives and interests resolutely.

Do you think that conversations can't change the world? Within nine months, two women were appointed to national secretary positions in the Australian cabinet. Within five years, the group achieved its goal, and now there are seven women cabinet ministers. In other words, a group of leaders determined to shift a context overturned one hundred years of history in five years. The practice those leaders gained at context shifting helped them, furthered their cause, and spread their perspective to a like-minded network of supporters and contributors. The scale and impact of their work was magnified many times.

I ask you to undertake a groundbreaking project too because it will require you to shift context at many points along the journey to produce this audacious outcome. Your choice of project does not matter, except that it be near and dear to your heart and seemingly impossible to achieve from your current vantage point. In addition, it should be something that, once you look back on your accomplishment, you can safely say would not have happened if not for your vision. Notice that I'm not saying that you now have the authority or resources to accomplish it. In fact, it would better serve our purpose of demonstrating the power of the trade-up methodology if you aren't in a formal position to make it happen. Instead, you will need to change your own reality and the reality of others in order to get the job done.

What Future Could You Change?

If you're flirting with the idea of taking your leadership to the next level, and if the thought of a life in which your work is connected to things you truly believe in exhilarates you, then a groundbreaking project can accelerate your development rapidly. Contrast that with a project that has a predictable outcome and can be accomplished with no context shift or a stretch goal that can be produced with working harder or longer doing the same things you've always done. It's up to you to decide how you want to make a difference in the world. You may already know what change you want to create. But if you don't, then there is a process you can follow to get there. To identify a groundbreaking project, it helps to have a brainstorming session with your team, your enlisted supporters, or your closest allies. First, a definition: *Groundbreaking results disrupt and revolutionize the status quo, while being specific, measurable, and linked to your core vision.* (See Figure 5.5.)

You can think of your vision as the playing field in which you want to operate. Ask yourself, What legacy would I like to leave for my family, or my team, or my community, or even the world? That's the scale at which you can project your vision.

A groundbreaking project is a game within that field. It's important not to be paralyzed by the pressure of selecting the perfect vision, however. Any groundbreaking exercise will provide

Figure 5.5   Groundbreaking:
Beyond Predictable or Stretch

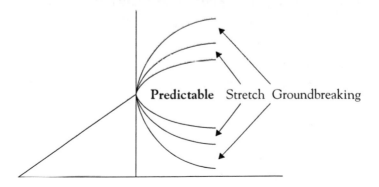

you with learning you can apply to all future projects. Remember, a groundbreaking project is an "unknown." The harder your project is, the more difficult it will be to articulate aloud, the more nervous you will be about not knowing how to do it, the more you'll sweat before you even begin to make it happen. Thinking about your project will involve pushing yourself and others out of binary ways of looking at the possibilities, defeating the tyranny of either/or thinking. You'll know you've encountered binary thinking when you start running into obstacles and hard choices, accompanied by the sounds of various committee members screaming in your head. There may be a sense that there is a lack of experience or practice, or an unwillingness to disrupt what exists. But groundbreaking change, by definition, means going places you and your team haven't gone before. You can't be fearful of taking risks or wait to gain confidence before proceeding.

A key decision to be made at the outset of your groundbreaking project is to determine whether your goal really is a groundbreaking one. You can ask questions like these:

- Is the outcome a clean break with the past?
- Does it produce significant returns in forwarding your vision?
- Does it leave you, your team, organization, or society in a new field of possibility or a new reality of what is possible?

In any project, there are predictable results and there are quantum results. Working harder gives you predictable results. Conventional projects with predictable results—albeit high-performance ones—are best achieved through conventional means. But conventional means will only use up resources if they are applied to groundbreaking objectives. You may need to change the rules of the game.

With Whom Do I Want to Play?

To select a group of committed contributors, you need to be active about inviting participation. Be specific about your vision and elicit concrete and authentic responses to that vision. In other words, you are not trying to convince or guilt someone into participating, nor do you want responses that are enthusiastic on the surface but lack commitment underneath. You need to clarify people's commitments by scanning for what they care about and how it relates to what you care about. Everyone is on high alert for signals about their own opportunity. As you steer each conversation toward commitment and action, you need to keep your eye on the big picture conversations that will move your project forward.

You're not a leader without followers. This doesn't mean you need to drag, coerce, or manipulate people into mimicking your new language or new way of being. Instead, you're inviting a community of innovators and early adopters to a culture or a lifestyle or a possibility of living that is robust and expansive. Each person you enlist and partner with becomes a member of a growing community of curious seekers. Redesigning your life requires a community for feedback and support. As a leader, you are in the business of continuously trading up even as you help others with their trade-ups. Together, there isn't anything we can't accomplish . . . and goodness knows there is so much left to do.

To create a feasible pathway for your groundbreaking project, start with the future state and work backward to the present. If your project is occurring to people as impossible or unfeasible, they'll do nothing. You have to shift your project from the possible to the feasible so people will jump. Together, you can create a laundry list of ideas for how to get the groundbreaking project accomplished. As leader, you need to identify the conversations that will give people the fastest traction to achieving the ultimate goal.

Achieving groundbreaking change requires that you and everyone you come to work with believes that the goal is possible and that it has enough relevance for them to impact their behavior. In leading such a project you will be facilitating conversations that spur people into action and develop relationships and commitment that can support the change. As leader, this means building on your skill at linking other's concerns and commitments to the

Figure 5.6   Expanding the Playing Field

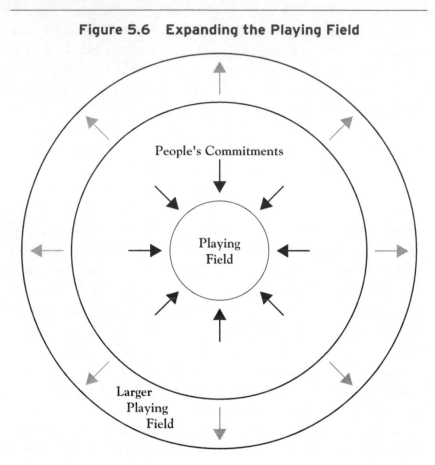

larger playing field that encompasses their work and mission, as shown in Figure 5.6.

The leader's job is to look for ways to expand the playing field larger than people's commitments. This is done through speaking and listening. Most people come to work and are given a playing field that is too small for their contribution. Trying to cram people's full contribution on too small a field results in turf wars, politics, and in-fighting. A groundbreaking project increases the field on which people can make their full contribution and thus enables them to exceed even the highest expectations.

Ask yourself and others these kinds of questions:

- What value does your project have across the entire spiral, ranging from the personal to the societal? Start with the personal (and repeat this with each person you enlist in your cause).
- How will you personally benefit by the successful completion of this project?
- What will it allow for or make possible for you?

Now scale up one level on the spiral.

- How will your team or group benefit from accomplishing the project goal?
- What will it enable them to do?

Now scale up again, ask the same questions about your organization and community. Finally, ask what benefit your project might have for humanity as a whole. You may be surprised by the answers. Using the matrix in Table 5.1, determine for which result you will register the value of that contribution. Put a name in the first cell section and then fill in the row using that name to fill in the blank.

Don't Let Red Rover, Red Rover Send You Back Over!

Once you choose to create a radical new playing field and make it real through your groundbreaking project, you need to stop the practices that allow the old context to get in the way of your progress. To do so, I recommend creating a three-column list, as shown in Table 5.2. In column 1, write down all the business challenges that you assume to be real, fixed, and immutable. In column 2, put the evidence or proof that the item in column 1 is a fact. Next, in column 3, write a new conclusion that replaces each item in column 1. Then, over the course of your project, track the number of times—whether in conversations, e-mail, or other communications—that you or someone else reinforces the old context in column 1.

Table 5.1 Registering the Value

Result	How will _____ benefit?	How will this result contribute to _____'s performance? What will this enable _____ to do, differently, more easily, better?	What will this result allow for, or make possible for _____? What is/are _____ positioned to do now?
You			
Team or Group			
Organization			
Customer or Community			
Customer's Customer, Society, Humanity			

Table 5.2 Redesigning "Reality"

Real, Fixed, Immutable Challenges	Proof	New Conclusion
_____	_____	_____
_____	_____	_____
_____	_____	_____

Each challenge you list is a reminder of the extent to which your prevailing context maintains its grip, even as it reinforces the importance of remaining vigilant and determined in your new practices. Set a goal either to stop or interrupt any conversation that represents those old conclusions as facts. You simply do not need to follow such roads any more.

Keep a Reliable and Timely Scorecard

It's important to set measurable objectives. A key factor in creating groundbreaking projects is setting the parameters accurately, rigorously, and with precision. Most companies register progress and success according to financial reports. Your scorecard will have a different frame of reference: *value*. Value, of course, is in the mind of those most impacted by the change. There's no such thing as objective value. There's only value that advances the commitments and concerns of the customer or individual you are trying to impact. Value is effort filtered through commitments and concerns. By figuring out the value your project has across the entire scale of the spiral, ranging from the personal to the societal, you can get an idea of the outcomes you want to see met along the way.

A common mistake is to assume that, because groundbreaking results are by definition beyond what is predictable, the setting of targets must lay somewhere between a leap of faith and an astrological reading. In contrast to this, your groundbreaking project requires scrupulous care and monitoring. The failure to set groundbreaking commitments accurately leaves your project with no platform for achievement.

Using your groundbreaking result as the focus of Table 5.3, answer the questions in the table. For example, the result will reduce the time to collect overdue accounts payable by 50 percent within thirty days. It will make a difference for the sales force. They benefit because they'll be paid their commissions in a more timely manner. It will advance their commitment to reconcile their commissions in a timely manner. It will address their concerns about how to manage their personal cash flow.

Table 5.3 Determining the Value

For whom would accomplishing this project make a difference?	How will he/she/they benefit, improve performance, or reduce costs?	How will it advance their commitments?	How will it address their concerns?

Victory Regardless of Outcome

The fulfillment of the groundbreaking vision will depend upon two seemingly paradoxical factors. First, you will see that the project participants working to achieve your targeted outcomes do so as though the objective matters to them as deeply as it does to you. Second, the project participants will come to recognize that what is at stake in the end is nothing short of the establishment of a new field of possibility. This means that the project team, especially as the project encounters unanticipated breakdowns and problems, will have to be able to adjust their sights and redesign any part of the project, including the targeted outcomes, without compromising the vision or losing their commitment. In the end, there will be two distinct questions to be answered to complete the project:

1. Were the targeted outcomes reached, not reached, or exceeded?

Figure 5.7   Creating the Future

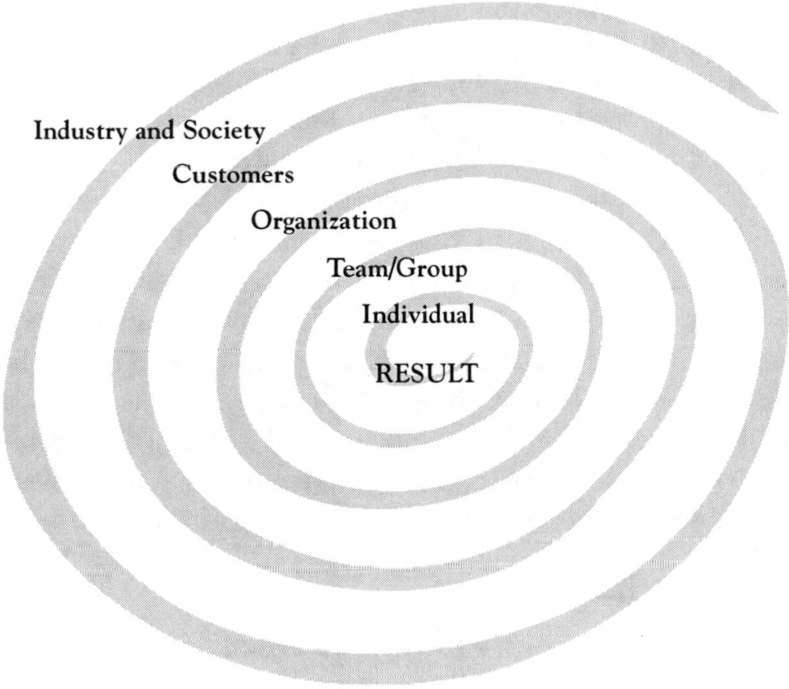

Industry and Society

Customers

Organization

Team/Group

Individual

RESULT

2. Is there a new future in place now that the groundbreaking result has been achieved? (See Figure 5.7.)

Gretchen McCoy's project team at Visa had a vision to create a new billing system for the entire organization. They succeeded in this vision, but as their measurable outcome of success they wanted to emerge from the journey with a strengthening of relationships within the team and the desire to do such work together again. They succeeded on that basis, too, making the entire project a groundbreaking one. That's the kind of sustainability and revolutionary result context shifting makes possible.

You're only limited by your willingness to keep inventing, to keep on shifting. The more you communicate about your project, the bigger your radar screen. Resources and people will start to show up in a way they didn't before. Then you'll know you're really on to something. Watch what happens when your dreams start coming true. You will find that achieving your vision happens much more rapidly than you can imagine. Breaking ground allows you to shift beyond incremental change to real, radical change. It allows you to orient yourself and your work from what's best in the world to what's best *for* the world.

Most of us are not aware of the impact our daily activities contribute to the greater good. How can one simple item on my "to do" list, like completing a project status report, contribute all the way out to the industry in which I work? While I cannot answer each of your questions specifically, I ask you to gaze at the spiral and keep asking yourself, "Who will benefit from what I am about to do, and how will they benefit?" Then ask yourself, "How will the benefit they receive also benefit others?" Before too long you will see that every discrete action has the potential to impact the world.

Outward, let the ripples spread.

Spreading the Word

Life is never boring once you have gained the capability of context shifting. There is always something deep and interesting to learn about others; there is always the opportunity to bring those people into your playing field, to align your interests and their interests, to take us all one step closer in fulfilling the reason why we are here in the world.

I once spent an afternoon at the Walk Through Time, a display sponsored by Hewlett-Packard's philanthropy group to illustrate the notion of the expansiveness of time. It's a one-mile walk past posterboards on stands, depicting the slightly more than 5 billion years of the Earth's evolutionary history. Each foot of the one-mile walk represents a million years. Near the beginning of the walk, we see a picture of a bacteria on the whiteboard. The land masses form. Eventually, as we near the end of our one-mile walk, the dinosaurs show up, then there is the rise of mammals. Finally, we come to *the last quarter-inch of the entire one-mile walk* and see the rise of human beings. One-quarter of an inch over one mile. That's not a significant amount of time cosmically speaking—in fact, it's an eye blink. And yet, consider how much has been accomplished during this eye blink. It's mind boggling to imagine.

What are you going to do during your own moment in the quarter-inch of time allotted to us? When you learn that it is possible to trade up to a new and more deliberate context, you recognize, perhaps for the first time, that you can live your moments awake at the wheel rather than asleep or dull to the scenery passing by.

Leadership is not a role, or a job, or a title; it's a way of dwelling in the world, a decision to be aware, intentional, active, and engaged. You can be drafted into so many roles in life, but you have to enlist in leadership, and that's what brings it closest to the urgings of your own heart. Why else, after all, would you bother to lead if not to release the ache that you feel for something lacking and make it come into existence? That's why leadership has to exist in the external world. It would be pointless to have a leadership transformation buried in the realm of your own psyche. The purpose of leadership is to manifest a vision, to create a game worth playing, to make something happen on your shift. We use the methodology of context shifting to express our leadership, so that we can leave the world better than we found it.

Epilogue

Ruminations and New Beginnings

Once we become aware of what we carry unconsciously, we can change. Change involves two things: awareness and action.

—*Riane Eisler*

I always wanted to be someone. . . . I just wish I had been more specific.

—*Lily Tomlin*

I love Lily Tomlin's quote because it reminds us all to be more discerning about our intentions. One of my favorite authors, Audre Lorde, said it beautifully in her book, *The Transformation of Silence Into Language and Action:*

> I was going to die, if not sooner than later, whether or not I had ever spoken myself. My silences had not protected me. Your silence will not protect you. But for every real word spoken, for every attempt I had ever made to speak those truths for which I am still seeking, I had made contact with other women while we examined the words to fit a world in which we all believed, bridging our differences.

> What are the words you do not yet have? What are the tyrannies you swallow day by day and attempt to make them your own,

until you sicken and die of them, still in silence? We have been socialized to respect fear more than our need for language.

When I dare to be powerful—to use my strength in the service of my vision, then it becomes less and less important whether I am afraid.

Trade Up! is a resource to help you find the words you do not yet have . . . the words that will allow you to redesign your leadership and life from the inside out. But of course there is a reason that we have two ears and only one mouth. We are meant to listen twice as much as we speak. When we listen both to what is said and what is unsaid, we distinguish ourselves as leaders. I've always been the type of person who would speak up and speak the unspeakable: "P-yew, does anybody else smell that dog poop. . . . Everybody check your shoes." This hasn't always made me popular but it has trained me to trust myself. If I'm saying it to myself, then at least some other people are saying it to themselves. As a child I always wondered why we never spoke about those family secrets. Years of therapy and thousands of dollars in self-improvement programs retrained me how to use my voice and articulate the things that were going on that no one was talking about. If you don't get anything else out of this book but the fascination, curiosity, and courage to put your context on loudspeaker so that you can have a choice about trading up, then I've done my job.

With any change of self comes the challenge of retraining your environment. Consider the possibility that you've already brilliantly trained all the people around you to relate to you as your inherited context. They are in a perfect dance with who you *used* to be. It will be disruptive to them for you to change. It changes the homeostasis of your relationship. I invite you to bring compassion and patience to the journey of retraining your community. Let it be fun. Find playful ways to talk about it and encourage others to explore the virtues of a traded-up relationship. Make amends for anything you've done while operating from your prevailing context that left others wounded or disempowered.

I'm still cleaning up messes from my childhood. It's part of the maturation process.

Remember that while many of the people profiled in this book have big jobs with big titles, this book is for everyone who has ever had a desire to make a difference at any scale. Whether that difference is a modest change in the way a department processes invoices or a Girl Scout troop leader who wants to change the way her troop awards badges . . . context shifting is an equal opportunity skill, available to everyone.

My dear friend and mentor Virginia Satir used to tell me that none of us received an adequate education in being human. Now that my daughter is a young adult, I can see how much I wish that I would have had more education in context shifting and being human before I became a parent. She turned out beautifully in spite of my default contexts. Yes, we all pass along our contexts to our children. Some of those contexts serve them well, and some are like an old moth-eaten coat that should have been thrown away years ago. If there is any legacy I'd like to leave for future generations, including my own daughter, it is this: Not every conversation makes a difference . . . but any conversation could. Talk isn't cheap unless you cheapen it! With awareness comes freedom. . . . With freedom comes power. May each of us use our voices to create a sustainable world in which we all thrive and cohabitate in peace.

If it happens on our shift, then we definitely had something to do with it.

Acknowledgments

The two most important people in bringing this book to fruition are Kathe Sweeney from Jossey-Bass and my phenomenal collaborator, Keith Hollihan. I will be forever in debt to them for their vision, generosity of spirit, friendship, and partnership.

Thank you to Rehka Balu, Margot Silk Forrest, Cheryl Dahle, Leigh Stevens, and Jeannette Nelson for the earliest versions of this book, which allowed me to think in new ways about what I wanted to communicate.

I would never have made the publishing deadlines if it hadn't been for Tammy Aramian and the staff at the Institute for Women's Leadership; thank you for the support, late night hours, and keeping the plane flying while I wrestled the final manuscript to completion.

I am forever indebted to the clients who allowed me to profile them in this book. Each of them is a powerful example of how ordinary people can produce extraordinary results. Their willingness to reveal the upsides as well as the downsides of their growth process shows the contribution that authenticity can make to others.

I have always been a voracious learner and have been enriched enormously by the following teachers: Iona Mowrer, Werner Erhard, Doreen Durney, Peter Koestenbaum, Fernando Flores, Virginia Satir, John Wooden, Richard and Ariana Strozzi-Heckler, Ellen Wingard, Catherine Parrish, and countless others.

Ever since I read Hillary Clinton's book, *It Takes a Village to Raise a Child,* I have been using the sentence, "It takes a community to grow a leader." I am the beneficiary of hundreds of people in my community who have sanded and polished me until my leadership star could brightly shine. I could fill a book with the names and specific contribution of those people. Instead I am hoping that they will feel acknowledged by the impact this book makes in the world, knowing that without each one of them it would not have been a complete tapestry.

Some times in the wee hours of the morning when I am saying my gratitude prayers, I reflect on the people in my life (many who are in more than one category following), and I ask myself, "How could I be so blessed to have so many great people love me?"

While I have no final answer, I do want y'all to know that I love and appreciate each and every one of you. . . . Blessings and gratitude to:

My family

My friends

My lovers

My sports teammates

My coaches

My teachers

My mentors

My students

My clients

My work colleagues

My classmates

My Family Camp partners

My Women's Leadership Board

My Women and Public Policy Program partners

About the Author

Rayona Sharpnack founded the Institute for Women's Leadership—an organization renowned for its groundbreaking work throughout the United States, Australia, and Canada—in 1991. Drawing from her successful careers in education, professional sports, and business, Rayona is an inspirational teacher, coach, and mentor for executives in Fortune 500 companies, government agencies, emerging businesses, and nonprofit organizations.

Rayona's masterful approach as a coach and educator helps her take very complex theoretical concepts and distill them down to poignant, relevant, and easily accessible learning distinctions—resulting in dramatically more effective leadership skills for her clients.

Rayona has presented her outstanding achievements in advancing women leaders and building high-performance organizations to prestigious institutions and associations such as Harvard University, Stanford Business School, University of California Berkeley business school, Mills College, State of the World Forum, the Canadian federal government, the Australian federal government, Leadership America, and the Professional and Business Women of California. National publications such as *Fast Company*, *Working Mother*, and the *New York Times* have showcased Rayona's leadership model; she has delivered hundreds of keynote speeches and designed conferences focused on the topic of developing extraordinary women leaders. Rayona is one of several featured authors of the groundbreaking book, *Enlightened Power: How Women Are Transforming the Practice of Leadership*.

In addition to numerous awards, Rayona's work has earned her an appointment as chairwoman of the Mentoring and Leadership Development committee on the Kennedy School, Women's Leadership Board at Harvard.

Rayona spends much of her free time playing sports. The crown jewel of Rayona's life is her daughter, Chelsea, age twenty, who inspires, challenges, coaches, and generally keeps her mom in a continuous learning mode about the power of win-win solutions.

Index

through embodied practices, 136–142
through help from others, 126, 153,
154
through self-care, 145–150

T

Tao Te Ching, 35
Thinking
about conclusions, 24
impact on making change, 3–6, 32
Tomlin, Lily, 193
Trading up
author's experience of, 13–19, 59–60
as choice point, 104
as common occurrence, 2
defined, 11–12
kaleidoscope image for, 33, 34
as ongoing process, 153–155
skills for, 33
stories of, 1–2
thinking as beginning of, 3–6, 32
See also Shifting context
Trainer, Susan, 147–149
Trust
and assuming positive intent, 94–96
continuum of, 84–85
and feedback, 92–94
listening to establish, 87–92
techniques for creating, 83
Twain, Mark, 103

V

Value, tracking, in groundbreaking
projects, 187–188
Vision, determining, 119–120

W

Watson, Nora, 1
Way of being
change as beginning with, 11
gap between doing and, 25–28
horses giving feedback on, 38–40,
43–44, 46, 52–53, 106,
107–108, 148
and presence, 58
Williamson, Marianne, 157
Wingard, Ellen, 15, 101, 150–151
Winters, Grace
background on, 74
context owned by, 77–79
impact of context ownership for, 80–82
prevailing context of, 75–76
Work/life balance, 146–147, 149–150

Y

Yoga, 45, 78, 139, 140–141, 151, 152
Yunus, Muhammad, 5, 6

Z

Zone, Fran, 112

CPSIA information can be obtained at www.ICGtesting.com
Printed in the USA
LVOW10s0239120214

373293LV00004B/11/P